Publisher's Message for
TIME BOMB

Today's cultural, social, economic, and political issues are shaping the world we Canadians will encounter in the future.

To shed light on these vital topics, Dundurn's *Point of View* books offer readers the informed opinions of knowledgeable individuals who are directly immersed in them. Our goal is to illuminate the choices before us.

We are committed to framing the hard choices facing Canadians and spurring democratic debate within our country. For over forty years our publishing house has been defining Canada for Canadians. Our *Point of View* books now take us further along this journey.

Each author of a *Point of View* book has an important case to make, with a definite perspective about the issue under examination. Some *Point of View* books are manifestos for action. Others shed light on a crucial subject from an alternative perspective. All are intended to challenge and refresh the thinking of Canadians engaging issues that matter to us as citizens.

Time Bomb by Douglas Bland brings into focus the urgency of addressing the rising combativeness of a growing cadre of First Nations militants who are discontented with the status quo and capable of taking direct action to change it. This reality has long been, in the author's own words, "a toxic topic in Ottawa." Silence hardly seems a solution for a democratic country.

Kirk Howard
President

A Note from the General Editor

In 2010 Douglas Bland sought to warn and instruct Canadians about the risks to our highly vulnerable country from militant First Nations groups who are well armed, aggrieved, and angry. He said "another scholarly paper about the critical situation would end up just like other reports that nobody reads." So instead, he wrote a fast-paced work of fiction.

Setting *Uprising* in a near Canadian future "to reach as wide an audience as possible," he succeeded. As an internationally acknowledged authority on insurgency, Bland's compelling story became widely reported, including by Al Jazera, which viewed the warning soberly. *Uprising* was well reviewed by critics. It became the subject of conference presentations. A paperback edition was published. The novel was translated by Governor General Award-winning Michelle Tisseyre and published as *Soulèvement* in a French-language edition. Now it is the subject of a television series in development.

Lieutenant-Colonel Bland, free to speak as someone retired from military life, brings to this study his decades of service in the Canadian Forces, combined with his years as professor of security studies at Queen's University, his studies of First Nations conditions in Canada, advanced research into what triggers an uprising, and his understanding of the hard lessons about just how devastatingly effective a small band of determined and well-led rebels can be. Fearing many Canadians would dismiss armed insurrection here as implausible, I worked with Douglas Bland to create a website called "A Newsmakers Guide to *Uprising*." We filled it with extensive compilations of information across such categories as Housing, Employment, Education, Land Claims, Poverty, Literacy, Suicides, Protests, Demographics, and dozens more. The statistics, cases, and quotes came from authoritative reports by First Nations organizations, royal commissions, parliamentary studies, journalists, academic researchers, and judicial inquiries. Cumulatively, these factual reports on First Nations issues flashed like a red warning light.

This stunning composite about a Canadian reality proved that the issues Douglas Bland was identifying, and the catalogue of accumulated grievances by Canada's widespread and diverse First Nations peoples that he portrayed, are not fictional, even though in a novel. They are the real laboratory for something explosive.

Now, for Dundurn's new *Point of View* books, Douglas Bland crafts this shorter, *non-fiction* version of the compelling story all Canadians need to understand. As he said about *Uprising*, "If people do not like the way this turns out, then now is the time to act."

Time Bomb makes clear why time for curative action is on a short fuse.

J. Patrick Boyer
General Editor
Point of View books

TIME BOMB

Other *Point of View* Titles

Irresponsible Government
by Brent Rathgeber
Foreword by Andrew Coyne

TIME
BOMB

Canada and the First Nations

DOUGLAS L. BLAND

Foreword by Bonnie Butlin

DUNDURN
A J. PATRICK BOYER BOOK
TORONTO

Editor: Dominic Farrell
Design: Courtney Horner
Cover Design: Laura Boyle
Cover Image: Makarova Olga
Printer: Webcom

Library and Archives Canada Cataloguing in Publication

Bland, Douglas L., author
        Time bomb : Canada and the First Nations / Douglas L.
Bland ; foreword by Bonnie Butlin.

(Point of view)
Includes bibliographical references.
Issued in print and electronic formats.
ISBN 978-1-4597-2787-8 (pbk.)

        1. Native peoples--Canada--Government relations.
2. Ethnic conflict--Canada--Forecasting. I. Title.
II. Series: Point of view (Dundurn Press)

E78.C2B55 2014   305.897'071   C2014-906625-2

1   2   3   4   5   18   17   16   15   14

We acknowledge the support of the **Canada Council for the Arts** and the **Ontario Arts Council** for our publishing program. We also acknowledge the financial support of the **Government of Canada** through the **Canada Book Fund and Livres Canada Books,** and the **Government of Ontario** through the Ontario Book Publishing Tax Credit and the **Ontario Media Development Corporation**.

Care has been taken to trace the ownership of copyright material used in this book. The author and the publisher welcome any information enabling them to rectify any references or credits in subsequent editions.

J. Kirk Howard, President

The publisher is not responsible for websites or their content unless they are owned by the publisher.

Printed and bound in Canada.

VISIT US AT
Dundurn.com | @dundurnpress | Facebook.com/dundurnpress | Pinterest.com/dundurnpress

Dundurn
3 Church Street, Suite 500
Toronto, Ontario, Canada
M5E 1M2

This book is dedicated to Dr. Cori Schroder, my wife and companion, for her patience and assistance in driving this project to completion and also for her many insightful explanations of the realities of life on-reserve gained from those years of her profession life spent living among the First Nations people in Northern Ontario.

CONTENTS

FOREWORD

In this much-needed examination, Douglas Bland's *Time Bomb* brings a new perspective of the increasingly fractionalized relationship between First Nations and non-Aboriginal Canadians. *Time Bomb* explores the historic development of this relationship and its current manifestation as a "First Nations society within a larger Canadian society," within the context of current global and policy trends. The current relationship is no longer sustainable, in particular for the First Nations, who have experienced demonstrable social and economic disadvantage relative to the non-Aboriginal population. The First Nations and the Canadian government have reached an impasse, however, on how to transform the relationship, with First Nations calling for recognition of their inherent right to self-government, while the government is unwilling to cede sovereignty to First Nations. The impasse is such that even solutions, such as the proposed 2014 act on Aboriginal education, have themselves generated new grievances. Reliance on political willingness to consult with First Nations and on the Supreme Court of Canada have largely proven to be ineffective in moving the relationship between First Nations and non-Aboriginal Canadians forward from dialogue towards a truly integrated and productive relationship.

Not only is this fractionalized relationship worsening, but emerging economic trends and policies beyond the relationship itself, such as the current Canadian push for increased natural resource extraction and trade, are converging and may act as catalysts to generate a tipping point within the relationship. Jurisdictional control of the land remains largely undetermined and at issue. Canada's transportation and energy infrastructure — the backbone of the country's natural resources trade — overlays or borders on many of these Aboriginal and disputed lands. With Canadian natural resource development, extraction, and trade representing 25 percent of Canadian GDP, the security of transportation and energy infrastructure is critical. Canada's transportation and energy infrastructure has considerable vulnerabilities: it covers vast distances, has limited redundancy and multiple choke-points, and is susceptible to cascading effects should disruptions be sustained or widespread. Its vulnerability and the resulting risk to the Canadian economy is significant, and sustained disruption would have catastrophic effects within a matter of weeks.

Time Bomb proposes that the motivation-focused lens of greed and grievance theory that has been favoured by policymakers and academics, and in military and security doctrine, may no longer be the best fit for the First Nations-Canadian relationship, as motivations have become increasingly blurred by outside special interest groups. Cambridge academic Paul

Collier's Feasibility Theory is proposed as a new lens through which to approach the relationship. In this approach, the focus is more on risks and vulnerabilities than on motivations. Feasibility Theory highlights five determinants that, if present, could support conflict within a state. Bland suggests that all five determinants are present within the Canadian context, and that the Canadian government has some measure of control over only three of them, and therefore, improving the relationship with First Nations should be urgently prioritized.

Bland argues that as peaceful calls for transformation from First Nations continue to yield little in the way of results, and as the federal government and law enforcement agencies continue to monitor the situation with watchful restraint, there is an increasing openness to non-formal means of protest and negotiation among Aboriginal communities. *Time Bomb* suggests that there is a small but critical window of opportunity for both sides to defuse and de-escalate tension within the relationship, through reducing First Nations grievances, minimizing Canadian economic and infrastructure vulnerabilities, closing the social and economic gap between First Nations and non-Aboriginals, and engaging in a focused, strategically-flexible effort toward achieving a negotiated solution prior to violence erupting.

Bonnie Butlin is an expert in security and intelligence. Co-founder of the Security Partners' Forum, she is also the managing director of the Canadian Security Executive Forum. Voted "one of the most influential people in security" by Security Magazine *in 2013, Butlin will be inducted into the International Women in Homeland Security and Emergency Management Hall of Fame in November 2014. Bonnie lives in Ottawa.*

A NOTE TO THE READER

Broad studies of "the Aboriginal in Canada" can be found in other sources, though there is much concerning Aboriginal legal and social issues that still needs to be researched. This examination of Canadian-First Nations relations will touch here and there on "Aboriginal affairs" and generalized Aboriginal statistics to make, for instance, comparisons between the distinct Aboriginal communities. Most often, the references to the circumstances in the Métis and Inuit and Innu communities in the context of broader Aboriginal issues and policies occurs simply because the federal government and other sources often provide only consolidated information on Aboriginal affairs and policies. In some cases, I have relied on generalized Aboriginal information and statistics because statistical data specific to the First Nations and the factors important to this study were not otherwise available.

In most cases, the text, where it refers to Native Canadians, follows today's generally accepted forms and simply refers to the First Nations by their traditional band identification — the Roseau River First Nation, for example — and to the collective as "the First Nations" or some such construct. Nevertheless, depending on the sources used or consulted, the text might occasionally use terms such as "Native" or "Natives" or "Indian." In most places where the First Nations, Métis, and Inuit are being referred to together, the capitalized term "Aboriginal" will be used.

PREFACE

The central theme of this book is that if Canada's present policies and the historic indifference of Canadians toward the people of the First Nations and their aspirations continue without amendment, and if First Nations leaders continue to assert their right to unconditional sovereignty in Canada, then a confrontation between our two cultures is unavoidable. The critical questions for both societies in such a circumstance are: what form would such a confrontation take, and how widespread would it become?

It is overly strange, is it not, that Canadians today should find themselves enmeshed in an increasingly bitter, divisive, racial impasse. After all, Canada, as Canadians remind themselves incessantly, is a country that is respected worldwide for its tolerance and peacefulness. Canada is rightly acknowledged as a welcoming country for refugees from every region on earth; as a nation of peacekeepers and peacemakers; as the adversary of dictators and tyrants; and as a bastion of human rights. Canada is, the people tell each other, a champion of Native sovereignty in South Africa, and in the former prisoner states of the Warsaw Pact and in scores of other, now free, states. Canada, "the country that works," built on the rule of law, freedom of speech, fairness, and equality for all is supposedly a human rights example for the world.

How is it, then, if this image is true, that thousands of First Nations people and other Aboriginal people in Canada live in poverty, fill our prisons, and, obviously, are not equal before the law? How is it that treaties agreed to more than 150 years ago have yet to be honoured? How is it that Canada defends the sovereignty of far-off places of which most Canadians know little or nothing at all, yet stridently denies the sovereignty of First Nations whose homelands have never been surrendered to anyone? Why do the majority of Canadians hold in contempt First Nations people even though very few Canadians have ever seen or spoken to "an Indian"?

Perhaps the answers to these and other such questions reside in Canada's non-Aboriginal cultural and political history, a history, for all its honour and achievement, constructed on the founding idea that our European-based political ideas are obviously superior to those of "the others" — *"les sauvages."* From this perspective, it may seem reasonable to many Canadian leaders and citizens that the First Nations people who live within *our* borders should, for their own betterment, abandon their history, culture, and traditions and melt away into ours.

On the other hand, perhaps the problems arise simply because this small Native society within Canada's larger prosperous community is a stranger to most Canadians. The First Nations people and their communities, for the most part, are literally and figuratively isolated from the Canadian mainstream. The common interactions between Canada's society and this distinct Native society occur on the peripheries of both — we live together separately. This reality has had far-ranging and enduring consequences for Canada, as both societies continue their uneven evolution towards an unsure future, together or apart, in some yet-to-be-discovered communal order.

It might be helpful if Canadians understood how the First Nations people see themselves. To gain that perspective, however, it would be necessary to put the realities facing Aboriginal people in a context far beyond that presented in the daily news and the political rhetoric hollered from both sides. Gaining a sense of the reality faced year after year by thousands of First Nations people might result in the development of a sense of compassion for Aboriginals and their plight, though such knowledge seems rarely to achieve that; in fact, the usual non-Aboriginal reaction to media stories and reports about "the poor Indians" is cold indifference. Whatever the reaction of non-Aboriginal Canadians to the reality faced by Native Canadians is on an emotional level, it should be stressed that awareness of the situation and the grievances of most First Nations people and their communities ought to be important to Canadians. To be blunt, grievances can lead to rebellions, whereas the compassionate redress of these same complaints *might* lead to a more peaceful and profitable relationship of all.

Unfortunately, the Canadian/First Nations relationship today is a very complicated one, and improving it will require more than a simple matter of recognizing and redressing grievances. The reality today is that this is a relationship challenged by increasing impatience everywhere within the First Nations community and growing cynicism in mainstream Canadian society toward First Nations complaints and demands.

Canada's relations with the First Nations (2011 population: 851,560), are unstable and potentially dangerous, therefore, of urgent importance to both communities. Canada's relations with the other so-called "Aboriginal people" — the Métis (451,795) and the Inuit, including the Innu of Labrador (59,445) — present today no immediate danger. Although the Government of Canada and Statistics Canada and other researchers have their own reasons for grouping these people together, there is in fact no unified Aboriginal community in Canada. The various groups — and in some cases many First Nations — are distinguished from each other by their unique histories, cultures, languages, political ambitions, and, it cannot be denied, by their once (and, perhaps, still latent) inimical relationships.

Canada faces a variety of policy challenges involving its Aboriginal population — the First Nations, the Métis, and the Inuit communities, — but, as this study will show, the time bomb in our midst lies mainly in the hands of some people in some of the First Nations. It is not a danger born in or nurtured by the other peoples of the government-invented Aboriginal community.

CIVIL WARS AND CONFRONTATIONS

The concept of civil war might seem rather obvious, and at its simplest, it is: a civil war is an armed quarrel between organized groups of people in one political domain who fight each other for control of something. Yet, despite the seeming simplicity of the concept of civil war, the prevalence and critical importance of these wars over the last seventy years or so has led researchers to spend considerable time and effort trying to understand such wars better. This work has resulted in the creation of libraries of research into the causes, circumstances, histories, methods, and characteristics of this type of warfare.

Civil wars are referred to by a variety of names: rebellions, revolutions, insurgencies, insurrections. These terms, unfortunately, have little explanatory value; they do not in or by themselves convey much sense of the aims, means, or even the tactics of such conflicts or how one might avoid or resolve them. Over many years, politicians, soldiers, and scholars have attempted to clarify the term *civil war*, but generally they have failed to reach a consensus. The result is that particular civil wars have been described mostly in terms particular to how they are conducted.

There is a general agreement that three characteristics define most civil wars:

- First, unless they are meaningless slaughters, all civil wars have some political framework, and the aim is to destroy or defend a government's or faction's legitimacy, authority, and coherence through armed actions and/or through unarmed national and international political agitation.
- Second, as the British officer General Sir Rupert Smith argues, modern civil wars are best understood as "wars among the people … in which the people in the streets and house and fields — all the people, anywhere — are the [targets] and the battlefield."
- Third, civil wars are most often very bloody affairs, conducted with few restraints and fought almost entirely by people with very limited professional experience or training.

At the heart of the present disturbance, and possible future confrontation, between Canada's two communities is the question of who decides who gets what; in other words, it is an argument about sovereignty. From the perspective of most First Nations' leaders their people never surrendered their sovereignty. Today's disagreements result in large part from Canada's refusal to respect the Royal Proclamation of 1763, which established the boundaries for non-Native settlement in Canada and served as the base for subsequent treaties — these too have been largely ignored by Canada over the past one hundred years. Canada's failure to abide by the Proclamation and by its treaty obligations in effect stripped the Native people of their land — the foundation of their traditional ways of life — and thus, in the minds of Canadian politicians, abolished Native sovereignty. First Nations leaders in 2014 are determined to regain their lost sovereignty. Previous federal governments were as determined to maintain and enforce the indivisible sovereignty of Canada and the government today is no different.

Time Bomb is a facts-based essay meant to be read not from a First Nations point of view or as a prediction that an uprising is inevitable — it is not. Rather, the study is meant to serve as a barometer warning of stormy days — perhaps even catastrophic years — ahead for relations between the First Nations people and Canadians.

The possibility that our two communities will stagger into a widespread civil conflict, whether armed or unarmed, is worrisome. Making this possibility even more worrisome is the reality that (according to a recent theory on the causes of insurgency developed by scholars at Oxford University) "where a rebellion is feasible it will occur." The theory argues that feasibility is dependent on the presence of five "determinants" that are explained and placed in a Canadian context in Chapter 4. For now, it is important to acknowledge that the time bomb, unfortunately for Canada, is heavily armed by Canada's economic vulnerabilities — vulnerabilities that are almost impossible to lessen but easy to exploit.

The nation's economy, to a significant degree, is dependent on the export of natural resources and grain, which is in turn dependant on the country's unguarded transportation infrastructure. Any disruption of the national railway system, in particular, would harm these vital industries and would have, almost immediately, significant negative consequences for Canada's economic well-being. Most political leaders in Canada understand this precarious situation. And every First Nations leader recognizes Canada's economic vulnerability as well.

A Canada-First Nations confrontation can be prevented, but only by neutralizing the underlying determinants that make such an insurgency feasible in the first place. *Time Bomb* addresses this matter in detail and sets out for Canadians' consideration a "pre-emptive strategy" that might just help Canadian and the First Nations people avoid a "war among the people," and a tragedy for everyone and for the nation.

If so, Canada might be able to avoid the horrors that accompanied the great American disaster, "The War Between the States," a war delivered to the people of the United States 150 years ago by the rash actions of leaders of a profoundly divided, fractionalized nation. President Abraham Lincoln foresaw the dangers of this fatal flaw and on June 22, 1858, warned the American people of its consequences: "A house divided against itself cannot stand. I believe this government cannot endure, permanently half slave and half free. I do not expect the Union to be dissolved — I do not expect the house to fall — but I do expect it will cease to be divided. It will become all one thing or all the other."

America eventually became "one thing," but at the cost of 650,000 lives. Abraham Lincoln's words carry a noteworthy message and a warning for Canada and the First Nations, if they would simply take a moment to consider them and then think about where Canada — a house dividing against itself — may be headed.

1

AS NATIVE AS THE LAND ITSELF

ew Canadians outside of a small cadre of specialized scholars, subject-matter lawyers inside and outside of government, a few hundred Ottawa bureaucrats, federal and provincial politicians from ridings that include proportionally significant numbers of Aboriginal people, and the mayors and administrators of several large and medium size cities — Winnipeg, Saskatoon, Thunder Bay, and Caledonia, for example — know much about Native Canadians and their aspirations and challenges. On the other hand, federal and provincial police officers and the custodians of our jails and prisons are well acquainted with them.

The relatively small Native society that exists within Canada's larger society is a stranger to most Canadians for several reasons, but chiefly because most of the First Nations people and their communities are literally and figuratively isolated from the Canadian mainstream. The common interactions between Canada's society and Native society occur on the periphery of both — we tend to live together separately. This reality has had, and will continue to have, far-ranging and enduring consequences for Canada as both societies continue their uneven evolution toward an unsure future, together or apart, in some yet-to-be-discovered communal order. Ensuring that that new reality is a better one will be endlessly difficult, however, if Canadians do not understand who Native Canadians are.

THE ABORIGINAL PEOPLE

In 2011, more than 1.4 million people in Canada (4.3 percent of the Canadian population) identified themselves as Inuit, Métis, or First Nations; that is, as "Aboriginal" people. Between 2006 and 2011, the Aboriginal population grew by 20.1 percent. In the same period, the non-Aboriginal population grew by a mere 5.2 percent; in some regions of Canada, the non-Aboriginal population did not grow at all. The largest Aboriginal populations live in Ontario and the Western provinces. Measured by the percentage of the total population they make up, however, the most significant Aboriginal communities — politically and economically — inhabit the Prairie Provinces (38.5 percent), the Yukon (23.1 percent), the Northwest Territories (51.9 percent), and Nunavut (86.3 percent).[1]

Within the broader, *officially recognized* Aboriginal community, there are three groups that are commonly defined by Canadians and their governments as distinct populations: the First Nations, the Inuit, and the Métis. These divisions may seem rather straightforward and reasonable to most Canadians. In fact, since such divisions affect questions of identity, the situation is anything but straightforward:

> In a field of complex and contentious
> issues, understanding Aboriginal identity in
> Canada is one of the most challenging tasks.
> Perceptions of Aboriginal identity can be
> complex. Definitions may have legal impli-
> cations that often operate in surprising ways.
> [T]he various ways in which Aboriginal peo-
> ples in Canada self-identify and are defined by
> the state ... [create] two systems of definition,
> one based in law and legislation, the other
> in family tradition and community practice,
> [and these two] are frequently in conflict.[2]

Identifying people, and especially strangers, in a multi-ethnic society such as Canada, requires tact, nuance, and sensitivity. Terms, or labels, commonly used in past times to identify Aboriginal people might be considered entirely inappropriate and hurtful today. Many of these terms originated in and reinforced the history and culture of the European occupation of North and South America. For example, such terms as *Native*, *Indians*, and *Aboriginal* were used by European and American explorers mostly because they had meaning in the European languages and needed in most conversations or documents no further elaboration. In many instances, the situation is the same today. Try, for instance, to speak to a European, even a worldly one, about the state of "Canadian and First Nations relations" and you will likely have to stop and explain what "Canadian and Indian relations" means.

Until about 1990, many First Nations people seemed (admittedly from a non-Aboriginal perspective) unperturbed — or were they just politely silent? — when identified by other Canadians as *Natives* or *Indians*. But times change and so too do customs. Today, "identity politics" are more prevalent and not just in Aboriginal communities. First Nations people, and their leaders especially, today prefer to refer to themselves and their culture in terms specific to their heritage. Thus, First Nations people tend to identify themselves and their communities by nationality — as, for instance, Mohawks or Iroquois. Going further, the trend is increasingly to use traditional language names — in these cases: *Kanien'Keha:ka* and *Kanonsionni*.[3] These changes are important to the First Nations, not only because they more accurately identify the various clans, but also because these ancient languages and titles help to recapture the unique cultures and histories of the First Nations. Most importantly, they serve to define the exceptionality of the First Nations people among the vast host of immigrants in the so-called Canadian mosaic.

The term *Inuit* seems today to have been generally accepted across the northern community, perhaps because it is far less offensive than "Eskimo." Another benefit is that it has a more or less universal meaning in the languages of the communities of people in Northern Canada.

A Métis is a person who self-identifies as Métis, is distinct from other Aboriginal peoples, is of historic Métis Nation ancestry, and who is accepted by the Métis Nation.[4] In traditional Métis communities in Western Canada, the term is often used in a more restricted sense, to describe people of French-Indian ancestry who have a direct and historic connection to an identifiable historic Métis community, such as the Red River Métis community of Louis Riel. In 2013, the Federal Court ruled that 200,000 Métis are "Indians" under the Constitution Act, although what specific benefits will flow to the Métis from this ruling is, in 2014, still under review.

Although the federal government groups the First Nations, Inuit, and Métis (and always, it seems, in that order) under the jurisdiction of one cabinet minister supported by the Aboriginal Affairs and Northern Development Canada (AANDC) bureaucracy, it's important to keep in mind that these, are, in important ways, three "distinct societies." Though many of their concerns are similar, these communities, and at times bands and groups within them, often have unique histories, policy objectives, and grievances. Less well acknowledged by Native people in the company of non-Aboriginal people or parliamentary committees is the historic (and sometimes modern) animosity between these Aboriginal communities — Métis against Indians; Indians against Métis; and Inuit against Indians — that lies not too far beneath the surface and erupts, occasionally, when the interests of one community appear to favour or disadvantage one against the other.

THE FIRST NATIONS

Approximately 851,560 individuals or 60.8 percent of the total Aboriginal community and 2.6 percent of the Canadian population are *recognized* by the federal government as First Nations people. Within this community, some 637,660 First Nations people are reported as "registered Indians" (referred to at times as "status Indians"). Another 213,900 First Nations people identified themselves as "non-registered Indians." Registered or status Indians are individuals who are registered with AANDC as "Indians" under the terms of the Indian Act — the Canadian law governing First Nations people — and who, thus, have specific rights and benefits not available to non-status Indians. Among other things,

"Benefits may include on-reserve housing benefits, education, and exemption from federal, provincial, and territorial taxes in specific situations." AANDC administers the act and maintains and supervises the Indian Register. "The Registrar [an employee of AANDC] is the sole authority for determining which names will be added, deleted, or omitted from the Register."[5] In effect, who is an "Indian" in law is determined by the federal government and not necessarily by the First Nations people themselves.

Individual First Nations in Canada are set apart by their ancient cultures and histories and, more particularly, by the traditional concept of "bands" that identifies individuals as a member of a more or less distinctive group of people. This traditional identification has a longstanding legal meaning in Canadian law: "A band is defined as a body of Indians for whose collective use and benefit lands have been set apart or money is held by the Crown, or who have been declared [by the government] to be a band for the purpose of the Indian Act."[6] Individual bands can be quite small — 70 percent have fewer than five hundred inhabitants; others identify more than ten thousand people as members. Bands of the same ethnicity, even if scattered over a vast territory, might identify themselves as members of the same clan or culture as do, for instance, the Western Cree and the members of the Five Nations within the Iroquois Confederacy in Ontario, Quebec, and Northeastern United States.

Although, in 2014, the definition of a band in the Indian Act has not changed, a 1985 amendment to the act allowed Indian bands to exercise the right to establish or to elect to identify themselves a "First Nation" and change their band name to reflect such preferences. To add to the confusion (for non-Aboriginals at least) and difficulties in identifying

First Nations people as members of this or that band or First Nation, misunderstandings can multiply when the terms band and First Nations are used casually as synonyms and when, as seems common, either one or both identifiers may change over time outside of any formal process.

Some order is imposed on the situation by AANDC, which manages and registers the identification of bands and First Nations and insists that changes to band/First Nations names and changes to titles and definitions of First Nations and/or bands can only be made once each year. Nevertheless, anyone who decides to become deeply involved in "Native studies" or First Nations affairs had best be prepared to master a seemingly endless inconsistency in some band names and their spelling.

Some might argue that this social identification is not so very different from the modern identification of other people in the world, such as Canadians, Americans, or Italians, and especially of people in de-colonized nations. The distinction with respect to First Nations, however, is unique in the sense that while a Jamaican could become a Canadian, only in rare circumstances could a Mi' kmaq become a Cree or a Mohawk a Nisa'ga. In only the most unique circumstances could a non-Aboriginal person become a permanent band member anywhere in Canada.

The origins of the term *First Nation* is uncertain, but most accounts suggest that it became widely accepted in the late 1970s or early 1980s as a substitute for the unfashionable term, "Indian band." It has today generally replaced the term *band* in common usage, but not in a strict legal sense. It has also evolved to have a number of meanings: *a cultural meaning*, identifying a First Nations person; *a political meaning*, identifying a band or group of bands; and *a collective meaning*, identifying the entire population, as in "*the* First Nations" or a political organization such as "the Assembly of First Nations."

The term *nation* of course, when used nationally or internationally, especially in a political context, is much more powerful rhetorically than the term *band*, which has connotations of the primitive and a generally weaker sense to it. A nation from anywhere in the world, for instance, might seek membership in the United Nations — mere tribes or bands need not apply.

The issue of titles and names is not a trivial matter for the First Nations or for Canada. Bands defined and subordinate to the Indian Act are implicitly subordinate to the Canadian government. Today, in a legal (and oppressive) sense, they are "wards of the state." On the other hand, the acceptance of the title *First Nations* retrieves this subordinate relationship and carries it back to the early days of the British conquest of North America and the Royal Proclamation of 1763 when Crown and Aboriginal relations were more or less established — if not on an equal basis — on a nation-to-nation understanding. The effect of this twentieth century re-titling, as will be explored later in this book, is not inconsequential; it provides, arguably, a platform for the First Nations' claims to sovereignty in Canada.

A DANGEROUS HERITAGE

The "feasibility hypothesis" of insurgencies — as will be explained in detail in Chapter 4 — argues that a nation fractured by ethnic, social, and religious cleavages faces significant risk of instability and insurgency. "Fractionalization" is a major contributor to the feasibility of an insurgency, especially where the effects of this phenomenon are so obviously and deliberately brought down on the heads of particular members of a society. In Canada, three major issues define fractionalization between First Nations people and other Canadians: sovereignty; Canada's failure to complete or honour land claims and treaties; and social and economic grievances.

SOVEREIGNTY

The Indian Act and the long history of the intrusion of the federal government into every detail of First Nations' lives and traditions demonstrate boldly that in all matters related to First Nations the federal government is sovereign and the First Nations are subordinate. This fact is shown clearly in the matter of First Nations membership, arguably *the* defining criteria of national sovereignty. For instance, before the Indian Act was amended in 1985,

> ... Status Indian women who married non-Status men lost their Registered Indian status [and all benefits] and were ordered off reserves by chiefs and council. As well, these women could not pass their Registered Indian status on to their children. The opposite was true for non-status women who married Status Indian men. These women and their children were automatically entitled to Indian status.[7]

This gross inequality was deleted from the act in 1985. However, this change in the rules for First Nations eligibility status by the government was not, and apparently is still not, welcomed by some (usually men) in First Nations communities. After the act was amended by Parliament, some chiefs argued that the amendment usurped the band council's right to determine band membership and "…refused to reinstate expelled women."

A chief of a wealthy reserve in Alberta challenged the amendment in court, but it backfired. The court concluded "… that the Canadian government — not First Nations — had the ultimate say in determining band membership."[8]

Separate from the issue of who should decide a woman's *formal* status in this case is the issue of the *general* status of Native women. A woman's place on some reserves and in some Métis and Inuit communities is still not always a happy one. In light of the continuing resistance to change shown by some male Aboriginal elders, it should surprise no one to find that sexual prejudices not greatly different from similar prejudices resident in the rest of Canada persist in Aboriginal societies.

Beyond the issue discussed above, the questions of who is sovereign when and where and who commands Canada-First Nations decision-making and policy processes remain the most quarrelsome and sensitive issues facing the First Nations and the Government of Canada in 2014. The Constitution Act, 1987, recognized the First Nations' "inherent right of self-government." The application of that right, however, raises complex issues concerning community governance, federal funding, financial transparency, culture, traditions, education, and institutions, among other important matters.

As extraordinarily difficult as it may be to find agreement between all the First Nations and the federal government on these types of internal issues, self-government is even more of a legal jungle for Canada's federal and, to a lesser degree, provincial governments when questions of sovereignty arise.

How is the federal government to reconcile the concept of Aboriginal self-government with the overriding principle (in the view of Canada's federal and provincial governments) that Canada is unconditionally sovereign? The conundrum — as will be discussed later in this essay — for governments is how to place "safeguards" on the concept of First Nations self-government without impinging on the sovereign rights of the First Nations as they themselves see them.

So long as the apparent contradictions between the concept of Canada's absolute sovereignty and the concept of inherent rights of self-government persist, conflicts between Canada and the First Nations will erupt whenever the Government of Canada declares its authority over any policy area that First Nations leaders insist trespasses on their rights and domain. Of course, a confrontation could erupt if, for example, a First Nations attempted — or threatened — in the estimation of the government to arbitrarily broaden the boundaries of its right to self-government.

King George III, in his Royal Proclamation of 1763, declared that "… the several Nations and Tribes of Indians with whom We are connected, and who live under our Protection, should not be molested or disturbed in the Possession of such … reserves [ceded by the Crown] to them or any of them, as their Hunting Grounds." The Proclamation is today held by First Nations leaders as proof of their peoples' special relationship with the Crown and as evidence that their lands were never forfeited to any Canadian government, except where treaties were agreed to that effect. In 2014, the Canadian territory is divided, generally, between the state, land held by treaty, and land held by First Nations that was never ceded to Canada by treaty or otherwise. Few Canada-First Nations issues produce more confusion and legal and political rancour than does contests over who owns what in Canada.

LAND CLAIMS AND TREATIES

"Aboriginal title is a legal right derived from historic occupation of the Tribal lands by Native people. It is not something that was given to Native people by some government, by Royal proclamation, or by the signing of a treaty."[9]

The people of the First Nations in Canada are as native to the land as are the forests and the plains, the rivers and the lakes, and the birds, animals, and plants that have existed on the land for millennia. For the people, their indivisible harmony, their all-embracing sense of oneness with the living land, is a spiritual, not a physical phenomenon. The land is everything, but it has no economic value and cannot be owned or traded by an individual. For most non-Native North Americans, on the other hand, their sense of and identity with the land is of a starkly different personal nature, an attachment defined almost entirely in terms of ownership, intrinsic value, and/or political patriotism — "our home and native land."

Of course, the Native people of North America, both today and throughout their long history, certainly understand the concept of patriotism in terms of belonging — whether that sense of belonging is related to clans or bands or, more recently, to "nations." They understand well the politics of alliances and confederacies and fought wars with and against each other for trophies, and dominance, one over the others. Many of these contests, however, were motivated by their warrior cultures and the associated importance of displaying individual honour.

The clashes between Native populations and settlers from the time of "first contact" and on into the twenty-first century were not, and are not today, about "the land" as First Nations may see it; rather, these clashes — these political, often bloody, contests — have been almost entirely about a vision of the land as Euro-Canadians see it, that is: who *owns* the land.

Canada and the Aboriginal people are today engaged in negotiating modern treaties, comprehensive land claims, and specific claims. It is arduous work, but by 2014 the government has settled more than twenty-five comprehensive claims (including those with the Inuit and Innu nations) covering, by some estimates, 40 percent of Canada's land mass. Specific claims arise mainly from Canada's failure to honour previous treaties or obligations to the First Nations, Inuit, and Innu peoples. Here too, progress is being made.

Nevertheless, considerable treaty difficulties have yet to be redressed satisfactorily. In some cases, treaties concluded in the 1800s have yet to be honoured completely. Substantial amounts of money are on the table as are hundreds of thousands of acres of land. Several of these cases, however, have been stalled because the federal government withdrew from the entire process.

Other treaty-related difficulties are complicating the various processes. For instance, control over natural resources rights potentially worth billions of dollars is seen as increasingly critical matter for both sides. Also, the notion that the government has a "duty to consult" Aboriginal people as it develops policies and negotiating positions is a complicated business, especially when some Aboriginal people assume the principle to consult includes a right to veto government decisions and policies.

Canadians and the First Nations people are today engaged in political and legal battles that ultimately stem from the difference between the idea of land as Natives see it and the Euro-American idea of land as demarcated property. If this conflict of ideas is irresolvable or if peace will come only when one idea prevails over the other, then the future for one side, and more probably for both, is indeed threatening.

SOCIAL AND ECONOMIC GRIEVANCES

The social circumstances of most First Nations people is, indeed, appalling, but this is especially true for the estimated 35 percent of the population — nearly 300,000 individuals — who live on-reserve. The difference between the social circumstances of the majority of Canadians and the Third-World state of the people of the First Nations alone defines the fracture between the two societies. The detailed state of life for First Nations will be examined in Chapter 3, but at this point a brief summary of social issues and statistics will provide a sense of the divide between our two communities.

The First Nations population is young and growing rapidly — more than half of the First Nations, 415,000 people, are under fifteen years of age. They live, on-reserve, in "crowded housing" requiring "major repairs." More than 60 percent of First Nations children have not completed high school and never will. Most of the income for almost 45 percent of people, and especially for those on-reserve, comes from social assistance. Heart disease, diabetes, tuberculosis, and other infectious diseases are common health problems and some at near epidemic levels. Fetal Alcohol Syndrome is a serious and growing problem on most reserves caused in large part by alcoholism evident in all ages. Social depression, leading to violent behaviour and high rates of suicide, is a common malady in the community. Drug abuse, crime, and spousal and elder abuse characterize "normal life" on many reserves. Health care in most every case falls far behind care that is routinely available to Canadian citizens across Canada. Canada's jails and prisons are filled with the human remains of these circumstances. More than 70 percent of prisoners in federal and provincial institutions in western Canada are Aboriginal. Most are young men, but to the alarm of many authorities, the number of Aboriginal women in custody is increasing enormously.

The national fractures created by history, land claims, treaties and these dismal social facts of life may seem distant from the concerns of most Canadians, but obtaining a successful resolution for their historic and modern-day grievances and proper acknowledgement of their treaty rights are crucially important to Aboriginal people. As the true cost of today's and future treaties and settlements becomes known, a majority of non-Aboriginal Canadians may well recoil at the bill. Should the price for settling these treaties become the future focus of Canadian–First Nations affairs, the stability of the relationship maybe become very rocky, indeed.

These types of circumstances — hesitant dealing over self-government; deplorable and prejudiced social policies; and longstanding treaty violations by federal governments — create what some theorists claim to be the "root causes of insurgencies." The reliability of such theories will be addressed in Chapter 4, but the obvious fact is that Canadian and First Nations people are divided by the social and political conditions under which each community lives, and that divide provides the fuel that feeds resentment and hostility between the communities. The growing resentment among young First Nations people who decaled that they will be "Idle No More" suggests that sensible people on both sides should accept the necessity for deep, meaningful reforms to our relationship.

Canada in 2014 is a nation segregated not by accident, but, from its earliest days, by the will of Parliament. The consequences of settlers' unbridled intrusions into and occupation of Native lands, the roundup of the people and their confinement on reserves, and the imposition of the Indian Act to control and direct their every decision, among other abuses, were eighteenth-century outrages, even by the low standards of those times. The First Nations of the twenty-first century live with these burdens today.

The depth of this fracture between Canadians and the First Nations and the dangers that it portends for both communities demand that Canadians, for their own well-being, fundamentally reconsider the laws and national policies that allow this fracture to exist. Exploring these laws and policies is where this book will take us next.

2

THE CROWN'S PROMISE
AND THE INDIAN ACT

"To be honest … if you're going to talk about Indians
in contemporary North America, you're going have
to discuss sovereignty. No way around it."
— *Thomas King*[1]

"**F**ractionalization" is one of the five and is arguably the
most causal of the determinations underpinning the
feasibility hypothesis of insurgencies and civil wars. The establishment of the 1876 Indian Act, and the laws and policies
following from it, fundamentally "fractionalized" Canada into
two racially divided societies: the European settlers and the
Native Indians. Its harsh application created, and by many
accounts still creates, generations of misery and poverty for
the First Nations. Evidence to support this assertion resides
in the appalling circumstances under which Aboriginal communities exist even today, most of which can be traced to the
nineteenth century attitudes of the politicians and officials

who created — with the willing or absent-minded consent of most settlers and missionaries — the Indian Act.

The current state of Canadian-First Nations affairs cannot be fully comprehended, nor can a way forward be designed or implemented without reference to the Indian Act and its long unhappy history for the people of the First Nations. Moreover, it is unlikely that any resolution of the friction between Canada's fractionalized communities can occur without first understanding the remains of Canada's early settler history.

KING GEORGE III AND HIS PLEDGE TO THE PEOPLE

The relationship of the Aboriginal peoples in Canada with their governments — federal and provincial — is today founded on the Royal Proclamation, 1763, in which King George III declared:

> ... being desirous that all Our loving Subjects ... may avail themselves with all convenient Speed, of the great Benefits and Advantages which must accrue therefrom [the British conquest of North America] to their Commerce, Manufactures, and Navigation ... [the Crown establishes] the Laws, Statues and Ordinances for the Public Peace, Welfare, and Good Government of Our said Colonies and of the People and the Inhabitants thereof.[2]

The Crown's 1763 policy concerning the Aboriginal people of North America was, not surprisingly, self-serving. Nevertheless, it established in effect a treaty-based alliance with Canada's Native people premised on a principle:

> Whereas it is just and reasonable, and essential to our Interests, and the Security of our Colonies, that the several Nations and Tribes of Indians with whom We are connected, and who live under our Protection, [We declare that they] should not be molested or disturbed in the Possession of such parts of Our Dominions and Territories as, not having been ceded to or purchased by Us [the Crown], are reserved to them or any of them, as their Hunting Grounds.[3]

Thus did the Royal Proclamation confirm that the Native people who before 1763 occupied this newly conquered "Crown land" would, by the Crown's command, continue "at pleasure" to possess the land thereafter. To safeguard its policy, the Crown reserved unto itself the "Sovereignty, Protection and Dominion for the use of the said Indians" of all territories in what is today Canada. It also "strictly" forbade "on Pain of our Displeasure" any attempt by anyone to purchase or settle or possess any reserved lands. Furthermore, any person "who … either willfully or inadvertently seated themselves upon any [not ceded] lands" was ordered to "forthwith remove themselves from such Settlements."[4]

The Crown, however, anticipated that at some future time the status of the "not ceded land" might change and acted:

first, to protect the Crown's privilege to acquire such lands; and second, to make such transfers from the Native people to the Crown transparent by regulation. Specifically, the Proclamation commanded that: "… if at any Time any said *Indians should be inclined* to dispose of the said land, that same shall be purchased only for Us [the Crown]." The implication of these policies is that the Native lands not ceded or sold to representatives of the Crown at the time of the Proclamation were deemed as remaining "property" of the various Native groups. And, arguably, these lands remain so today.[5]

This declaration lies behind all of the land claims disputes between First Nations and the government. "[L]and claims [in the modern era] arise from one of two circumstances: the Crown's failure to fulfill its obligations according to the terms of a specific treaty; or its failure to abide by the terms of the Royal Proclamation." Such failures might include a failure to set aside land to which a First Nation is entitled or the use of Native land for any reason without first obtaining "informed consent" from a First Nation in possession of the land. Such failures "give rise to comprehensive land claims" that can result in negotiations and modern treaties.[6]

All treaty-making in Canada is based on the Royal Proclamation's three central concepts: recognition, respect, and consent. These few but fundamentally important concepts, set out by the Crown within months of acquiring the Canadian colonies, have, arguably, "… been the foundation of treaty-making in Canada since 1763."[7] They provide the unalterable foundation of Canada's fundamental relationship with and responsibilities to the Aboriginal people in Canada.

No one should consider the Royal Proclamation as merely a quaint relic handed down by an ancient, now irrelevant monarchy.

Rather, Canadians should consider the Proclamation's fundamental concepts as important guides to understanding how we — the First Nations people and Canadians — might together enhance our potential as a society now and into the future. As a start, it is necessary for non-Aboriginal Canadians to accept their present-day responsibility to respect "the good-faith acceptance" by the Aboriginal leaders in 1763, who assumed, as present-day First Nations leaders do, that the Royal Proclamation was an unalterable statement of the Crown's continuing relationship with and its obligations to the First Nations.

Unfortunately, since the establishment of the Confederation Act, 1867, not only have the principles set out in the Royal Proclamation not formed the basis for Canada's dealings with the First Nations, they have in almost all respects been thrown aside. The relationship of mutual trust and respect established in 1763 was destroyed in 1876, when the now dysfunctional Indian Act was passed by Parliament. Under the rules set up by the act, modern day governments have been able to dictate a relationship with Canada's Aboriginal people of inequality and dependence. If Canadians are to avoid the consequences of a confrontation between our peoples, then Canadians must retreat from this perilous practice and embrace once again the founding concepts at the heart of the Royal Proclamation.[8]

THE INDIAN ACT, 1876

"The Indian Act tried to displace [overnight] ways of life that had been in place for generations; tried to wipe away the promises of Treaty that we would respect one another and share, that we would not impose one way of life over another. All these [Indian Act] experiments were utter and abject failures."[9]

— *AFN Chief Shawn A-in-chut Atleo*

Canadian policies regarding the First Nations never were and are not today constructed on the principles of "recognition, respect, and consent." Rather, they were and are constructed on the idea of European racial superiority and policies aimed at assimilating the First Nations into the developing Canadian culture — a policy that was claimed, at least rhetorically, to be for their own good and welfare, of course.

The Indian Act of today is an act of Parliament, derived for the most part from the consolidation of earlier colonial legislation such as the Gradual Civilization Act, 1857, and the Gradual Enfranchisement Act, 1869. These acts were intended to confer on First Nations full Canadian citizenship in exchange for the surrender of their "status" as Indians and all the rights that accrued to them as a result of such official identification by the government. However, such attempts at voluntary enfranchisement were largely failures. At the time, the requirement that a person be able to speak, read, and write English excluded many; more importantly, though, voluntary enfranchisement failed because First Nations people were not willing to surrender their culture, ways of life, or their tribal identities for the dubious right of citizenship. The Indian Act was designed to try to change this situation. It consolidated the earlier acts but also aimed, as Prime Minister Sir John A. Macdonald declared, "… [at doing] away with the tribal system and assimilating the Indian people in all respects with the other inhabitants of the Dominion as speedily as *they are fit to change.*"[10]

Today, as in 1876 and despite several amendments, the Indian Act retains its central purpose and remains a commanding fact of life for on-reserve First Nations people. It dictates every facet of governance and public administration on all reserves. The act places the present and future of on-reserve people in the hands of the minister of AANDC, "… the superintendent general of Indian Affairs," who is the sole authority and final arbiter should any question concerning the application of the act arise. The obvious conclusion is that First Nations people who live on-reserve are for all practical purposes wards of the state placed under the care of this minister of the Crown.

The act, just over 135 years of age, in the view of most First Nations leaders and reasonable Canadians, is a paternalistic and authoritarian document that makes plain the intended guardian-dependant relationship. A few *diktats* taken from the document highlight these criticisms and exemplify the intent of the whole.[11]

> **[Section] 5.** There shall be maintained in the Department an Indian Register in which shall be recorded the name of every person who is entitled to be registered as an Indian under this Act.

> **[Section] 20.** No Indian is lawfully in possession of land in a reserve unless, with the approval of the Minister, possession of the land has been allotted to him by the council of the band.

[**Section**] **32.** A transaction of any kind whereby a band or a member thereof purports to sell, barter, exchange, give or otherwise dispose of cattle or other animals, grain or hay, whether wild or cultivated, or root crops or plants or their products from a reserve in Manitoba, Saskatchewan or Alberta, to a person other than a member of that band, is void unless the superintendent approves the transaction in writing.[12]

[**Section**] **34 (2).** Where, in the opinion of the Minister, a band has not carried out the instructions of the superintendent ... the Minister may cause the instructions to be carried out at the expense of the band or any member thereof and may recover the cost thereof from any amounts that are held by Her Majesty and are payable to the band or member.

The act also specifies how the chief and council will be elected. Unless the minister decides otherwise, the council of a band "... shall consist of one chief, and one councillor for every one hundred members of the band, but the number of councillors shall not be less than two nor more than twelve and no band shall have more than one chief." Not surprisingly, the governance model more or less replicates a typical British (and today Canadian) municipal or town structure. However, this structure was based on concepts that, in 1879, were largely unknown to the First Nations.

The governor-in-council (Section 74.4) can also decide how elections are conducted and establish "electoral sections," roughly akin to the ridings in a Canadian federal election, and "make regulations with respect to meetings to nominate candidates; the appointment and duties of electoral officers; the manner in which voting is to be carried out; election appeals; and the definition of residence for the purpose of determining the eligibility of voters." These electoral regulations common to Westminster-based democracies are, then and now, intended to bring a high degree of predictability to election procedures, and the Ottawa government was determined to entrench this system in the Indian community.

The Indian Act was part of the "settler government's" grand national strategy aimed at imposing on the First Nations a foreign system of laws and governance so as to reshape fundamentally their societies and their ancient ways of life. In these matters, the government was eagerly assisted by the clergy of various denominations and by popular non-Aboriginal opinion in Canada in general.

From the earliest days, First Nations communities resisted the government's attempts to overthrow their traditional ceremonies and their internal economies. Governments, however, had huge advantages in terms of money, organization, and law-making powers. Deployed across the country, the government's "Indian agents," were empowered to arrest and jail anyone they suspected of contravening any section of the Indian Act. The agents, reinforced by various police forces and local military militia units, were backed by federal and provincial courts and magistrates.

The government's most powerful and effective weapon, however, was its control of the funds, food, and other resources that were provided to people on-reserve. These necessities were carefully managed by the Indian agents, who decided how those resources were to be used. In most cases, because their traditional economies had been deliberately destroyed by the reserve system, the First Nations people knew that they would face serious difficulties if such resources were withdrawn. So, for the most part, they acceded to the demands of the Indian agents. Indeed, as James Daschuk explains in detail, in 1878 government officials "in Western Canada ... quickly turned to the food crisis [starvation on reserves] as a means to control [the First Nations] to facilitate construction of the railways and opening the country to agrarian settlement."[13]

REFORMING THE INDIAN ACT

As Canadians gradually became aware of the poverty of many reserves and as the shortcomings and harsh unfairness of the Indian Act became more and more difficult to ignore, federal politicians grudgingly looked for ways to amend the act. The first major reforms were enacted in 1951, and other incremental changes have followed since then. The majority of these amendments have followed not from some public demand for just treatment of First Nations, however, but mainly from court decisions and other quasi-judicial rulings. These periodic amendments to the act have reformed such things as the rights of Aboriginal women, voting rights on and off-reserve, some aspects of band governance, and the regulation of band memberships.[14] While these changes have resulted in improvements, it should be noted that all such amendments and changes to the act and their implementation and supervision have, of course, remained in the hands of "… the superintendent general of Indian affairs," who throughout colonial and Canadian history has always been a non-Aboriginal person.

Since 1951, there have been several attempts to enact comprehensive reforms or to repeal entirely the Indian Act. Efforts have also been made to close completely Aboriginal Affairs and Northern Development Canada. All such attempts have failed.

The most ambitious reform, at least in the view of Prime Minister Pierre Trudeau's government, was the 1969 White Paper "Statement of the Government of Canada on Indian Policy" put forward by Jean Chrétien, then Minister of Indian and Northern Affairs, INAC. It proposed a repeal of the entire Indian Act and, consequentially, the end of federal responsibility for First Nations and of "special status" for Aboriginal people. For the government, it seemed a way of achieving "the end of the Indian problem." It was, in effect, another detailed plan for the final assimilation of the people of the First Nations into Canadian society. The entire plan and program were "overwhelmingly rejected by the First Nations."[15] Several other such attempts have been advanced in Parliament since then; all have "died" in the House of Commons or the Senate.

Meanwhile, efforts to reconcile the Indian Act with twenty-first century circumstances continue. In October 2012, Member of Parliament Rob Clarke introduced his private member's bill, C-428: the Indian Act Amendment and Replacement Act. Clarke's bill was intended to review all sections of the Indian Act and remove from it sections that are "paternalistic and unjustly deny certain Indians from enjoying the same rights as other Canadians." The bill, if it became law, which is unusual for a private member's bill, would amend or repeal more than twenty sections of the act and radically change the formal relationship between Canada and the First Nations.[16]

It was almost immediately, and for several familiar reasons, labelled by many in the First Nations community as a covert attempt to change radically the Indian Act. A number of First Nations organizations criticized the government for its "complete lack of consultation" that preceded the introduction of the bill in the House of Commons. As well, the suggestion that C-248 might be accepted if it received support from "First Nations organizations that have demonstrated an interest in the [bill]" and "other [unidentified] interested parties" was attacked as an attempt to divide the First Nations community.[17]

Other Native leaders, such as British Columbia chief Jody Wilson-Raybould, agreed with Mr. Clark that the First Nations "… need strong and appropriate governance … [but] tinkering with the Indian Act [merely creates] an illusion of progress." In her April 2013 presentation to the House of Commons Standing Committee on Aboriginal Affairs and Northern Development, Chief Wilson-Raybould reminded the committee that the "First Nations do have solutions and are making progress in their efforts to move away from the Indian Act [and] we need to continue developing *our* solutions, building on *our* success and what we have learned over the past forty years from the First Nations that are already governing outside the Indian Act." She emphasized that Bill C-248 "… is not a mechanism that would move us closer to the appropriate legislative framework that would assist our Nations in comprehensively moving beyond the Act."[18]

Wilson-Raybould's remarks were not a plea to hold tight to the status quo; rather, she appealed to the committee for the inclusion of First Nations in any process meant to construct a new regime to guide Canadian and First Nations relations in the future.

Perhaps the strongest rejection of Bill C-248 came from Shawn A-in-chut Atleo:

> We all agree we need to move away from the Indian Act, but any efforts must be led by First Nations and done with First Nations, not for First Nations. Moving beyond the Indian Act is about ending unilateral approaches by government and supporting and empowering First Nation governments to drive solutions in ways that respect and implement their rights, responsibilities and decision-making. This work must be done on First Nations terms. The way forward is about First Nations driving solutions and implementing approaches that work for our peoples and communities.[19]

Year after year, the First Nations continue to reject governments' attempts to amend the Indian Act, a frustrating roadblock that prompts many Canadians to ask an obvious question: Why does the federal government not simply repeal the act and negotiate a modern conceptual framework to guide Canada's relationship with the First Nations? This often asked but still unanswered question exposes the central paradox in the Canada-First Nations relationship today.

No one likes or can defend the Indian Act as it now stands. As Pierre Trudeau attempted to do in 1969, most every Canadian prime minister would like to repeal the act or otherwise settle once and for all "the Indian problem" so that we can all go about our national business. Harold Cardinal, a well-respected First Nations leader, agrees that a better arrangement needs to be found, but, he explains, unless certain conditions are met, the First Nations need and will continue to defend the status quo Indian Act:

> We [First Nations] do not want the Indian Act because it is good legislation. It isn't.... But it is a lever in our hands and an embarrassment to the government.... [W]e would rather live in bondage under the inequitable Indian Act than surrender our sacred rights [implicitly guarded by the act]. Any time the government wants to honour its obligations to us we are more than happy to devise new Indian legislation.[20]

The difficulty for Canadian governments is that First Nations leaders today reject the historic model for the Canadian-First Nations relationship in which the federal government is sovereign and the First Nations are not. They insist that "... if any alternative political relationship is to be worked out between First Nations and the government, First Nations will need to be active participants in establishing it.[21] In other words, *before* the commencement of any negotiations aimed at reaching a new "political relationship" with the First Nations, Canada would have to recognize the sovereignty of the First Nations

— individually or as a whole — and engage them from this uncompromising platform in "nation-to-nation" negotiations.

Here then is Canada's national dilemma. If Canada were to concede a pre-existing right of sovereignty to the First Nations, what defence would Canada have against Quebec's longstanding claim to the same thing? The proposition is so fraught with dangers to Canada's sovereignty and so likely to threaten the unity of the nation that no such approach would ever be contemplated by any federal government. It would seem, therefore, that some type of incremental dismantling of the Indian Act in all but name is the least dangerous, though still not uncomplicated, of the few constitutional options available to Canada and the First Nations in 2014.

THE INDIAN ACT AS A RELIC

Most reasonable Canadians would agree that establishing a just, comprehensive, and uniform governance agreement between Canadian governments — federal and provincial — and Aboriginal people is the indispensable foundation for "Public Peace, Welfare, and Good Government" in Canada in the twenty-first century.[22] Building such a unique regime would be complicated; indeed, perhaps impossible if based on a foundation of ideas and assumptions created in and for a vanished era. Continuing to tinker with the Indian Act will likely only frustrate any new attempts to modernize Canada-First Nations' relationships. Leaders on both sides need to embrace the idea that fundamental transformation must be at the centre of any endeavour meant to create together a peaceful future relationship for Canada and the First Nations.

Fortunately, the building blocks for this transformation are being assembled now, even if unevenly and without a master blueprint of the future relationship.

CONSTITUTION ACT, 1982, SECTION 35

First among these building blocks is the Constitution Act, 1982, Section 35. It confirms that "[T]he existing Aboriginal and treaty rights of Aboriginal people of Canada are hereby recognized and affirmed." The act "for greater clarity" confirms also that "… 'treaty rights' includes rights that exist now [in 1982] by way of land claims agreements or may be so acquired." Of great significance in 2014 and in any future Canada-First Nations negotiations, the Constitution Act, 1982, Section 35 also commits the Government of Canada "… before any amendment is made … to section 25 of the Constitutional Act, 1867 to convene a constitutional conference to which the Prime Minister … will invite representatives of Aboriginal people to participate in the discussions on that item."[23]

This last principle is the basis for what the Supreme Court of Canada declares is the federal government's duty to take the initiative to consult with Aboriginal communities prior to government decisions that might affect Aboriginal rights. This duty was established by the court to encourage Aboriginal and non-Aboriginal communities "to find paths towards reconciliation" whenever they are confronted by questions of "rights" or "treaty rights." The duty does not entitle any First Nation to a legal veto power over government policies but, rather, it provides a way to establish if such policies or actions by the government might create an adverse impact on "asserted Aboriginal or treaty rights." The duty also obliges governments to act in good faith and to acknowledge issues and rights discovered through the consulting process.[24]

In 2014, Canadians watched this complexity in action as the federal government's attempts to introduce major changes to legislation dealing with the education of First Nations children fell apart because, in the opinion of some chiefs, the government had failed in its duty to consult the First Nations community.[25]

THE INHERENT RIGHT OF SELF-GOVERNMENT

The second element of transformation is the inherent right of self-government, a principle recognized by the Canadian government when it patriated the Constitution:

> The Government of Canada recognizes the inherent right of self-government as an existing Aboriginal right under section 35 of the Constitution Act, 1982. It recognizes, as well, that the inherent right may find expression in treaties, and in the context of the Crown's relationship with treaty First Nations. Recognition of the inherent right is *based on the view* that the Aboriginal peoples of Canada have the right to govern themselves in relation to matters that are *internal to their communities,* integral to their unique cultures, identities, traditions, languages and institutions, and with

respect to their special relationship to their
land and their resources.[26]

As important as inherent rights are, they are not unlim-
ited rights. No federal government would allow a multi-
nation sovereignty regime to develop in Canada: "Aboriginal
governments and institutions exercising *the inherent right* of
self-government will operate within the framework of the
Canadian Constitution." In the opinion of the federal government, "[T]he inherent right of self-government does not
include a right of sovereignty in the international law sense,
and will not result in sovereign independent Aboriginal
nation-states."[27]

FIRST NATIONS GOVERNANCE

First Nations governance is the third critical building block
essential to any transformation of Canadian-First Nations
affairs. In the federal government's view, the central objective of its negotiations with First Nations will be to reach
agreements on self-government without being forced to
agree to legal definitions of the nature of inherent rights.
The government realizes that Aboriginal governments and
institutions will require the authority to act in a number
of areas in order to give practical effect to the inherent
right of self-government, but it prefers to try to limit that
authority. Broadly stated, the government views the scope
of Aboriginal jurisdiction or authority as likely extending
[only] to matters that are internal to the group, integral to
its distinct Aboriginal culture, and essential to its operation
as a government or institution.[28]

URBAN RESERVES

Urban reserves, another potentially transformational initiative, may be, as the federal government claims, "… a quiet success story."[29] Defined as "a reserve within or adjacent to an urban area," urban reserves provide First Nations people access to most of the economic and social amenities common to Canadians living in or near medium to large urban communities. More than 120 such reserves have been developed across Canada under the Additions to Reserve Policy and Treaty Land Entitlement Act. Most of these reserves were established through some type of legal settlements of specific land claims and treaty settlements.[30]

Put simply, the process results in the trading of land now "owned" by non-Aboriginal peoples or communities in exchange for the monetary equivalent of the present day market value of the land. Such payments, and they can be very large, *extinguish* future land claims, and allow First Nations to purchase new land that the federal government *may* transfer to reserve status "whether the property is located in an urban or rural setting."[31]

The central and unchanged concept carried forward from the Indian Act is evident in the federal government policy guidelines concerning urban reserves. The basis for those guidelines is the concept that the federal government, alone, is sovereign in matters of "Aboriginal affairs." Thus, again, as with the Indian Act, it is the government, through its agent, "… the superintendent general of Indian Affairs" (today the minister of AANDC) and not the First Nations community, that continues to define and to change from time to time the governance structures and the fundamental policy choices for First Nations. However, the government's authority will be restrained in the future, both by the Supreme Court of Canada–mandated principle of the duty to consult, and, as more urban reserve land claims are finalized, by treaty rights.

LIMITED SELF-GOVERNMENT

The federal government developed a comprehensive series of so-called self-government agreements with specific First Nations intended to establish "… one means of building sound governance and institutional capacity that allow … communities to contribute to, and participate in, the decisions that affect their lives and carry out effective relationships with other governments."[32] These types of "comprehensive agreements" — Canada has agreed to some thirty such agreements to date — give First Nations people greater control and authority over a number of fundamental community policies including, for example, governance, education, health, and environmental matters.[33]

Perhaps the most significant of such agreements was the 1984 Cree-Naskapi (Quebec) Act that freed the Cree on James Bay from the Indian Act and created the Cree Regional Authority that today manages, in partnership with the Government of Quebec and other entities, the giant Hydro-Québec James Bay facility.

SECTORIAL NEGOTIATIONS

Sectorial negotiations are another form of self-government and provide yet another route for First Nations to escape, in limited ways, the all-encompassing Indian Act. These negotiations allow the federal government in co-operation with specific self-selected First Nations to develop the capacity to govern one or two specific jurisdictions — for instance, land management, property ownership, fiscal management, oil and gas management, and commercial and industrial development. Under such arrangements, the governance authority of band councils is broadened to include other, specific jurisdictions, while leaving the participating band otherwise subject to the Indian Act. In effect, sectorial arrangements are the product of government negotiations with an individual First Nation, resulting in the voluntary and very specific and limited surrenders of government authority with respect to particular sections of the Indian Act arranged so as not to compromise the integrity of the act itself.[34]

AND SO, WHERE TO FROM HERE?

In 2013, Shawn Atleo declared: "The very earliest interactions between Indigenous peoples and Europeans within the territories of what is now Canada were characterized, for the most part, by mutual interests and respect. Relationships [were] established and based on recognition and respect ... the bedrock of the foundation upon which Canada is built."[35]

Are Canadian-First Nations relationships today based on "recognition and respect? And if relationships are not based on "recognition and respect," what then is the "bedrock" of Canada's relationships with the First Nations?

As they consider this question, it is important that Canadians understand that the difficulties and deep discontent that arise today between Canada and the First Nations cannot be resolved without reference to the social and political fractures born in the nation's colonial history. It is important also that Canadians understand and accept that these fractures are a major cause of an increasing number of disputes between First Nations and the federal government. Although we might hope that these disputes will be resolved through political accommodation or through the courts, Canadians need to consider the consequences that may arise if for whatever reason these approaches fail.

Canada, today and into the foreseeable future, is to an overwhelming degree dependent economically on the export of natural resources, a business that is inescapably dependent on Canada's vulnerable rail and road transportation systems. Most of these resources are located in Native or disputed land, and all of the transportation networks pass through these lands also. Should we fail to find together reasonable ways to resolve the underlying causes of the fractures and frictions in our community, some Native people may simply abandon conversations and the courts and instead seek redress to their grievances through "activist tactics," to everyone's discomfort.

3

LIFE AMONGST THE PEOPLE

"For many First Nations people in Canada, but especially for women and children, life on-reserve is dreary, dark, and dangerous."[1]

Nowhere are Canadians and First Nations people as "fractionalized" as they are in their comparative social-economic circumstances. Whereas Canadians live proudly in one of the safest, most hopeful, and healthiest societies on earth, a majority of the First Nations people live in downtrodden despair in the most shameful "Third World" conditions one might imagine.

The people of the First Nations recognize and resent the inequalities between Canada's two communities, and many leaders are, rightfully and aggressively, demanding change. If a satisfactory series of wide-ranging social and economic policy reforms enacted by the Canadian government to narrow the fracture between our two societies do not appear very soon, then the several thousand of the generation under thirty years of age who make up the potential members of the First Nations "warrior cohort" might simply attempt to narrow the divide themselves. Canadians need to understand that they can do that more easily than most citizens might think possible.

With that warning in place, it is important to acknowledge that while life on most First Nations reserves is indeed "… dreary, dark, and dangerous," there are among the 2,700 reserves stories of success and well-being. In these communities, responsible leaders are emerging, healthy and prosperous communities are flourishing, and positive partnerships and economic relationships are developing between First Nations people and their neighbours in nearby towns and municipalities.

This new environment is evident not only in the well-established reserves in Ontario and Quebec and Alberta, but also in Yukon and in the northern regions of the western Prairies. Of special note is the continuing trend for First Nations people to go far "beyond the Indian Act" and take charge of their communities' governance. These initiatives vary from simply taking the settlement of reserve and band affairs out of the hands of the federal government, choosing instead to live locally and govern locally.[2] Increasingly, too, First Nations are taking control of economic development. The stimulant for all sides to build a new future working together is the promise of wealth based on the exploitation of both Native skills and Native-controlled natural resources. In many cases, businesses and development projects are being initiated and managed by First Nations leaders who are displaying growing confidence in their own entrepreneurial skills.

Canadians should celebrate these First Nations successes and support them. They must , however, also face directly the darker side of our relationship with the country's Aboriginal population and its consequences. The critical issue confronting

Native and non-Native governments alike is not the success of a score or more First Nations, but what must be done by Canadians to help First Nations leaders rehabilitate their failed and failing reserves and nations. Canadians cannot help to redress these problems if they remain ignorant of the true state of life in many First Nations reserves and the equally crippled state of the many thousands of First Nations people, especially young people, living off-reserve in our towns and cities.

I hope that readers will absorb the information and the facts here presented without immediately forming opinions as to causes. Neither should they be too hasty to put forward a hostile or a Samaritan's hand. There will be time in these and the following pages to take a stand as you will. It is important that you see the facts, but it is more important that you look beyond the facts and the written words and try to see the reality — the everyday squalor, the run-down houses, the kids high on drugs, the sick, untreated elders and babies, and the everyday violence of life on-reserve. See, as well, the lost young Native women prostituted in our cities, the kids lured into criminal gangs, and inevitably sentenced to a life in and out of Canada's jails and prisons. Perhaps, then, mainstream Canadian and First Nations leaders will understand that they are not facing a political question: Who is to blame? Or a constitutional question: Who is to decide who gets what? But rather, they are together facing an ethical question: What is the right thing to do in the reality we live in today?

HOME, HOME ON THE RESERVE

The First Nations population is very young and growing at an explosive rate. These facts have significant implications for a wide range of Canada's future policies, including its national security policies. Between 2006 and 2011 the growth rate in the First Nations population was estimated to be an astonishing 22.9 percent, or 156,525 persons. That is more than 5 percent above the theoretical "natural birth rate" and a consequence of a never-seen-before coincidence of a very low mortality rate and a very high fertility rate in the First Nations community.[3]

The median age in the First Nations community is twenty-six years of age (YOA) while the median age for non-Aboriginal Canadians is forty-one YOA. Of significant policy concern is the fact that 415,600 people or 48.8 percent of the First Nations population are under the age of twenty-four; 258,000 or 30 percent of the children are under fourteen YOA; and approximately 160,000 people or 18.4 percent are between fifteen and twenty-four YOA. In the non-Aboriginal population, on the other hand, the corresponding percentages are 29.5 percent, 16.5 percent and 12.9 percent.[4]

At the present growth rates — and there is no evidence that they are declining — Canada by 2017 could have 500,000 First Nations under the age of twenty-four. In the Prairies — the region with a very large First Nations population — it is estimated that by 2017 about 42 percent of the First Nations population will be under thirty YOA compared to less than 20 percent in this age group in the non-Aboriginal community in Canada. "Warrior cohorts," whether formed for military units, criminal gangs, or insurgent bands, are typically recruited from this 15–24 YOA population and led by "experienced" men and, occasionally women, from the 24–35 YOA cohort. In any community, it is the young people, especially poorly educated young people, those "left behind" or otherwise comparatively disadvantaged, who provide the main cadre for criminal and other anti-social activities. The First Nations community in 2014 is a classic example of this phenomenon.

Nearly half (49.3 percent) of First Nations people live on-reserve, and for most young First Nations people there, the prosperous, First-World Canadian experience is always far beyond the horizon. Life on-reserve often begins in a home defined by Statistics Canada as "crowded housing," that is, a house occupied by more than ten people. The typical on-reserve dwelling is a simple rectangular, wood-framed, one-storey bungalow constructed on an above-ground wooden foundation. It may or may not, depending on the particular reserve, have running water, electricity, and a source of heat other than a simple wood stove. There is a high (45 percent) probability that the house will require "major repairs" to its basic structure and its water and sanitation systems. By Canadian standards, about half the houses on isolated reserves would likely be condemned as unfit for human habitation.[5]

EDUCATION

Many larger First Nations maintain adequate primary schools on-reserve, and an estimated sixty First Nations post-secondary institutions deliver adult upgrading, as well as trades and apprenticeship, and diploma programs to an estimated ten thousand students; however, the educational achievements of children in most First Nations communities is at best disappointing and at worst an imminent Canadian social and security disaster. Most reserve schools are under-funded, and lack anything near modern facilities or permanent, well-trained teachers. The educational results produced in these circumstances speak for themselves.

According to the Assembly of First Nations, in 2012, "61 percent of First Nations adults [20–24 YOA] have not completed high school, compared with 13 percent of the non-Aboriginal people in Canada."[6] Statistics Canada reported in 2011 that although 44.8 percent of First Nations people aged twenty-five to sixty-four had a post-secondary degree, diploma, or trades certification, 64.7 percent of non-Aboriginals in the same age group had such qualifications.[7] It is not surprising to learn as well that in 2011 only 8.7 percent of First Nations people had a university degree, compared to 26.5 percent of the Canadian population.[8] Also not unexpected given the social conditions on most reserves, Statistics Canada reported in its 2013 *National Housing Survey*, that "[T]he proportion of First Nations people with post-secondary qualifications was higher among those without registered Indian status than those with status" and that "among status Indians" the proportion of college and university graduates was highest among those living off-reserve than those living on-reserve.[9]

Several factors contribute to the educational underachievement in the First Nations. Evidence, for the most part, points to insufficient infrastructure and capital support from the federal government as a chief cause for this outcome. For example, leaders reported in 2012 that 47 percent of First Nations need a new school; approximately 74 percent of existing schools require major repairs or upgrades, including such the provision of such basic things as clean drinking water; and more than half the schools have no gymnasium, kitchen, science laboratory, library, or educational technical support.[10]

The lack of funding to correct these failings and the lack of federal government consultations with First Nations leaders are major problems and central irritants in First Nations/

Canadian relations. Prime Minister Harper's government responded to this problem and introduced into Parliament in March 2014, the First Nations Control of First Nations Education Act, intended to put substantial new funding towards First Nations education and give more control over education into the hands of the community.

However, the provisions of the act and, especially, the way in which it was developed immediately caused ruptures, not only between the First Nations and the Government of Canada, but also within the First Nations and the Assembly of First Nations. Within days of the prime minister's carefully staged public announcement of the act, several prominent chiefs denounced the entire package of reforms and funding. They complained publically and harshly about National Chief of the Assembly of First Nations chief Shawn Atleo's complicity, as they saw it, in designing and agreeing to the education policy without the chiefs' authorization. Consequently, Chief Atleo resigned and Mr. Valcourt, minister of AADNC, put the legislation "… on hold until the AFN clarifies its position," a possibility that could take months, if not years, before it appears.[11]

EMPLOYMENT

The poor economic situation of many reserves is aggravated by the negative social circumstances of individuals and their communities. Although the source of income for nearly 55 percent of the First Nations population, on and off-reserve, is paid employment, the remainder of the community depends mostly on income from social assistance and child tax benefits. No matter the source of income in the Aboriginal community, however, average incomes are significantly lower than income in the non-Aboriginal community. First Nations people on-reserve (in 2005) had a median income of $14,000, while those living or employed off-reserve had a median income of approximately $22,500. In general, the median income for males is higher than for females regardless of Aboriginal identity.[12]

Given the fragile economies of Aboriginal communities, the so-called economic turndown of 2008 had a significant effect on the employment. "In the core-age working population (25–54 YOA) [full-time] employment fell by 2.8 percent in 2009 and by another 4.9 percent in 2010." In the non-Aboriginal community, employment fell by 1.7 percent but rebounded by 0.08 percent in 2010. More distressing is the fact that "the participation rate" for core-aged Aboriginal workers in 2010 was just 75 percent, whereas the rate for non-Aboriginal workers was 86.7 percent, "… the largest [gap] between these two groups over the four-year period for which comparable data exists." Young people aged 15–24 were particularly hard hit in this period as their participation rate declined by 5 percent, a full two percentage points greater than for the same demographic group in the non-Aboriginal community.[13]

HEALTH & WELL-BEING

First Nations people differ from the majority of Canadians not only because of their distinctive history and culture, but also because of their undeniable poorer state of physical and mental health. The long-term state of an individual's health, including mental health, is determined by many interrelated factors, including, among others, family health history, community customs, money, access to health care professionals and services, examples set by relatives and the community, and by feelings of security and well-being.

In the First Nations community, heart disease is 1.5 times more common than in the non-Aboriginal community; rates for Type II diabetes are three to five time higher; and tuberculosis is eight to ten times higher. Heredity can be a factor in cases of heart disease, but in the First Nations population obesity is also a significant cause : "Twenty-six percent of youth aged 12–17 were more likely to be overweight or obese than their non-Aboriginal counterparts (19 percent)."[14] Smoking and exposure to second-hand smoke are also serious contributors to heart disease, and approximately twice as many First Nations people smoke as do non-Aboriginal people. This results not only in increased rates of heart disease amongst the smokers, but also elevated rates amongst First Nations children, in comparison to non-Aboriginal children, since they are more often exposed to high concentrations of second-hand smoke. As a result of their increased exposure to smoking in the adult population, First Nations children are also more likely to take up smoking at a very young age.[15]

Several community factors common to First Nations put residents at greater health risks than people in non-Aboriginal communities. For example, the high rates of TB (tuberculosis) — "eight to ten times higher" than in the non-Aboriginal community — increases the chances of a First Nations individual being infected with TB, developing "active TB," and spreading it to others. An infected person may have a weakened immune system, which increases the risk of developing other debilitating illnesses. The fact that most First Nations people on-reserve, including the vulnerable young children, live in "crowded housing" with poor hygiene conditions, and have access to only limited medical services, greatly increases the risk of contracting communal tuberculosis.[16]

Diabetes is also a serious community health problem among First Nations individuals living on-reserve (and, to a lesser extent, among those off-reserve). The disease occurs at a younger age in the community than in the non-Aboriginal populations and "gestational diabetes" also occurs among females at a younger and higher rate than in the non-Aboriginal community. According to Health Canada, "the socio-cultural, biological, environmental and lifestyle changes seen in the First Nations, Inuit and Métis populations in the last half century have contributed significantly to increased rates of diabetes and its complications."[17]

Injector drug use is identified as the primary cause of exposure to HIV/AIDS in the Aboriginal communities where infections are another serious health problem. According to Canada's Public Health Agency, "Aboriginal people are over-represented among HIV and AIDS cases in Canada." The agency estimated in 2008 that "… Aboriginal people made up 8 percent of all [Canadians] living with HIV (including AIDS)." AIDS infections are growing as well and make up an estimated 3 to 4 percent of all such cases in the country. As with diabetes, infections appear at a younger age and in women more often than in the non-Aboriginal community.[18]

Mental health issues are of growing concern in First Nations communities, both on- and off-reserve. Although many of the difficulties facing the people are more or less the same as the mental difficulties afflicting other Canadians, some are rooted in cultural aspects unknown to those from outside the Aboriginal community. The most striking of these is the community-wide trauma inflicted on the First Nations by the

Residential School System of the last century. Health Canada reports "… that 75 percent of the case files from a sample of Aboriginal residential schools survivors contained mental health information with the most common … diagnoses being post-traumatic stress disorder, substance abuse disorder, and major depression."[19] Other causes for mental distress include poor education, lack of money and opportunities, substandard living conditions, domestic violence, and isolation.

These and other stresses already mentioned have had predictable, negative effects in the communities for many years. Thirty percent of First Nations people exhibit signs of deep depression. "Suicide and self-inflicted injuries are the leading cause of death for First Nations youth and adults up to forty-four years of age." Young people "… commit suicide [at a rate] about five to six times more often than non-Aboriginal youth." The suicide rate for First Nations males is 126/100,000 compared to 24/100,000 for non-Aboriginal males. For females, the suicide rate is 35/100,000 compared to 5/100,000. "The suicide rates for Inuit youth are among the highest in the world, at eleven times the national average."[20]

Alcohol, or rather the abuse of alcohol, is a continuing intergenerational difficulty in the First Nations community on and off-reserve. Although "the drunken Indian" is, perhaps, the most commonly held negative stereotype of Aboriginal people in Canadian society, the truth is that the problem is more nuanced than this common and unfair stereotype suggests. According to studies conducted by the Office of the Chief Coroner of Ontario (2006–2008), "First Nations are more likely to abstain from alcohol use than the Canadian population at large." He states that while about 80 percent of the "general [Canadian] population" reported using alcohol in the previous year, only

66 percent of First Nations people did so. Moreover, "after sixty years of age, the use of alcohol in First Nations drops to less than half the rate of Canadians on average."[21] This Ontario finding of social moderation in the use of alcohol in First Nations is supported by a 2013 Statistics Canada study. "Health at A Glance" found that 29 percent of First Nations people consumed no alcohol "in the past year" of the study, compared with 24 percent of non-Aboriginal people who did not.[22]

Two critical factors, however, disturb the Coroner's relatively positive picture. First, alcohol consumption in remote reserves tends to be higher (75.7 percent of individuals reported consuming alcohol) than in non-isolated reserves (64.6 percent). Second, the consumption rate in the communities is not at the heart of the security/social/health problems caused by alcohol in these communities. The devil is in the bottle. Many Native men and women typically engage in — and become addicted to — heavy binge drinking.[23] The consequences of this alcoholic behaviour, on-reserve and off-reserve, is family violence, child abuse and abandonment, spousal abuse, unemployment, increased petty crimes, and consequent frequent interventions by the police leading to criminal charges and imprisonment.

Alcohol abuse by Native women is very often unintentionally visited on their newborn children. Fetal alcohol syndrome (FAS), a birth defect caused by the mother's use of alcohol during pregnancy, is a serious health problem in First Nations communities. Newborn children who suffer from FAS may display, among other symptoms, poor growth while in the womb, low birth weight, and, after birth, decreased muscle tone and poor coordination, heart defects, facial deformities, developmental delay, learning difficulties, behavioural problems, and serious disciplinary and social abnormalities. These character-istics are more or less permanent and in the most severe cases result in life-long disabilities requiring the constant supervision of the affected individual. The risk of FAS can only be avoided if pregnant women abstain completely from any consumption of alcohol of any kind throughout their pregnancy. Embedding this message in many Native communities is difficult, however, since, by some reports, heavy binge drinking by women of all ages is commonplace.

The second complicating factor is that because of increased birth rates and declining rates of mortality, the average age of the Native population is declining. This is true as well for the present, fast-growing female population on the majority of reserves. The median age of females is now 27.7 YOA, and within this group, nearly 20 percent are between 15–24 YOA. By some estimates, the total First Nations female population in 2017 could be as high as 430,000 persons, with an estimated 86,000 of these 15–24 YOA.[24] If the present alcohol-related circumstances continue unchecked and if the future population estimates are even near to being accurate, then FAS-related casu-alties in the Aboriginal population could climb sharply. This would present every Canadian government and First Nations leader with a very worrying scenario: communities with a large, continually growing population of young, severely crippled FAS children who will require complex and expensive health and social welfare support for decades, if not for their lifetime.

The amount and quality of health care and social assistance available to children and senior citizens in the First Nations is a constant source of concern and frustration for First Nations leaders, especially when compared with the aid usually avail-able in the non-Aboriginal community. Rather than improving services to reserves, however, governments frequently elect to remove needy individuals in order to give them care and support in existing facilities off-reserve.

For children, this "solution" has especially dire results. According to AANDC, in 2011/2012 close to nine thousand children were removed from reserves and placed "in-care" across Canada.[25] Critics of the present system point to the lack of funds and to the sometimes confused divisions of responsibilities between the federal and provincial governments that produce this situation. "At the heart of the problem," some say, "is the fact that the federal government's budget for children's services in First Nations communities is at least 22 percent less per child than what the provincial governments dedicate for child welfare services in other communities."[26] The disparity in funding and the high cost of providing support to small and remote First Nations communities results in "... the removal of children from their families ... [something that] has become commonplace for underfunded child welfare services that lack the resources to intervene in other ways."[27] "In-care" treatment typically results in the separation of children from their Native communities and appears to have very harmful social effects. In many cases, it leads young people from foster care to a failed life within criminal gangs.

The federal government's position is that it has increased in-care program funding to $618 million in 2011–12. This funding, however, is directed mainly to cover inflation: the rising cost to maintain each child — a cost that is rising significantly as the number of "special needs children in-care" grows. Unfortunately, merely adding more dollars to this program neither significantly improves the quality of the care offered through such programs nor does it reduce the number of children that must be removed from reserves or the negative effects associated with such removal.

The federal and provincial governments, to their credit, have initiated new programs and funding arrangements to try to redress the persistent difficulties in the current programs. For example, AANDC in 2007 joined the "Enhanced Prevention Focused Approach" (EPFA), a program already operating in some provinces. The EPFA aims at reducing through on-reserve programs the number of children who in distressed situations are removed from their communities. "Early indications" from most provinces show a decrease in case loads, an increase in families accessing the "prevention-focused services," and an increase in "kinship care" rather than off-reserve non-Aboriginal care.[28]

Health care for senior Aboriginal people is as complex as care is for young people, but changing the situation is often more difficult. First Nations seniors in cities tend not to use mainstream health care services simply because many of them "… don't trust the system enough to use it." Furthermore, the relationship between health care professionals and older First Nations people is often unintentionally inhibited by "deeply entrenched stereotypes" held by health providers who treat First Nations people. These factors sometimes result in medical professionals failing to consider adequately the background of these particular patients or in patients not understanding or following properly medical orders.[29]

Elders who have lived most of their lives on-reserve, especially in remote reserves, face unique difficulties if they are injured or become critically ill. Imagine, for instance, how seriously stressful it would be for an elderly person who most likely has never been separated from the reserve to suddenly, and without the benefit of a familiar caregiver, be placed in a small floatplane and flown for a few hours to a large city such as Winnipeg and, once there, be admitted to a large, confusing hospital where most everything, including the language, the food, and the people are foreign. The Health Council of Canada reported in November 2013 that federal and provincial health care systems routinely fail First Nations' elders:

> Vulnerable seniors are expected to navigate complex health care systems and government bureaucracies by themselves. Many are struggling with chronic illness and disability, living in poverty, and mistrustful of mainstream society. Unless there is a case manager, Aboriginal patient navigator, translator, other health care provider, or family member who actively coordinates and oversees their care, seniors are fearful and likely to experience problems when they travel for care. Nonexistent or weak links between services mean that frail, vulnerable seniors end up without support and at risk for neglect [on-reserve or off-reserve].[30]

Confusion about whether provincial health services providers or federal authorities are responsible for health services for Aboriginal people resident in the provinces often results in "frail patients [being sent] home to their communities without [medical staff checking to ensure] there are appropriate support services or home accommodations in place. The lack of consistent medical records is also a significant problem." These difficulties are aggravated by uncoordinated systems that often use different paper files and incompatible electronic processing and record-keeping methods.[31]

The federal government's First Nations and Inuit Home and Community Care program (FNIHCC) was created to work with First Nations to establish home and community care services, but it does not have, according to the Health Council report, sufficient capabilities to provide seniors with the services they need. "In addition, some communities accessing the FNIHCC program find it difficult to retain qualified nursing staff because some provinces pay a higher wage scale, and because it can be difficult to recruit nurses to work in rural and remote communities."[32]

Other services and medical support are problematic. "[S]ome provinces offer First Nations seniors the same access to home care services as to other people in the province; some provide access only for services not provided through FNIHCC, or have struck independent agreements with communities; and others do not provide any home care services at all." Where home care is not available on-reserve "… seniors may need to leave the reserve permanently in order to access provincial health care services." All these identified difficulties and overlapping authorities make seniors' lives difficult, and as the population grows and ages these difficulties will only become more acute.[33]

ILLICIT AND PRESCRIPTION DRUGS

Illicit drug use is widespread on many reserves. In a 2011 study based on a 2008–2010 national survey in First Nations communities, Health Canada reported that alcohol and drug use and abuse was considered by residents to be the number one challenge to achieving "community wellness" for on-reserve communities (82.6 percent of respondents). Housing (70.7 percent) and employment (65.9 percent) were considered the next most pressing issues.[34] Particularly alarming were related findings of high levels of illicit drug use and injector drug use by both male and females between the ages of fifteen and twenty-four — supposedly the community's leaders of tomorrow.[35]

Chiefs and other community leaders are begging for help. In 2009, for example, the *Nisnawabe Aski* First Nation in Ontario declared a "state of emergency," hoping to alert the federal and Ontario governments to the seriousness of their communities' drug problem. Yet the problem and its dread outcomes continue today. In early 2013, *Neskantaga* First Nation leaders in the same area placed its society on "suicide watch" after four suicides and twenty attempted suicides by young people, all related to drug use.[36]

In April 2012, officials from the Cat Lake First Nation in the same region reported that out of a population of seven hundred "… they collect five hundred needles a week through the [village] needle-exchange program." They have 172 adults on their list of addicts and another 250 are suspect. Everyone else on the reserve is either a child or an elder."[37] Other reserves in the same region are also faced with drug addictions — mostly for OxyContin pain medicine. The new national regulations intended to make the illicit use of OxyContin more difficult have apparently led to a new surge in illicit Tylenol drug use. First Nations leaders across Northern Ontario and elsewhere warn that "[W]e have reached a breaking point and our communities are under crisis. Our community is exhausted emotionally and physically as we try to pick up the pieces from these tragic events."[38]

Across Canada, the drug disaster migrates from the present lost generation to the future lost generation. Saskatchewan's chief medical officer emphasized that the First Nations' drug issue in that province is "… intergenerational and it's almost a family thing. And that's the real worry, because it means that the family themselves don't have hope and that they've given up on life."[39] Meanwhile, the political talk continues, strategies are concocted, meetings are convened, and the tragedy escalates.

CRIME & VIOLENCE

Social life on many reserves is defined by poverty and its consequences, the most tragic of which may be the violence inflicted by First Nations people on each other. Domestic and criminal violence is a major, complex problem on almost every reserve in Canada and among First Nations people living off-reserve in Canadian cities and towns. "Aboriginal people are two times more likely than non-Aboriginal people to experience violent victimization such as an assault, sexual assault, or robbery," and most violent attacks are committed against young people (15–34 YOA) by someone known to them, "… a relative, friend [!], neighbour, or acquaintance."[40]

The Aboriginal communities in Yukon and the other northern territories are among the most violent places in Canada. In 2005, violent crime rates there were "more than four times higher than in the provinces." In the Northwest Territories, the crime rate was 41,245/100,000 population, a rate 1.3 times higher than in Nunavut, 1.8 times higher than in Yukon, and three times higher than in Saskatchewan — the province (in 2005) with the highest provincial crime rate.[41] This trend continues. In 2009, "violence assaults" in the territories were recorded as 240/1,000 and spousal abuse was very high at

51/1,000. Other violent criminal acts continued to escalate across the Territories reaching, in 2009, as high as 190/1,000.[42]

A 2009 Statistics Canada study, *Violent Victimization of Aboriginal Women in the Canadian Provinces*, found that Aboriginal women between the ages of fifteen and thirty-four "… were almost three times as likely as non-Aboriginal women to self-report being the victim of a violent crime…." Most violent attacks — "beatings, sexual assaults, and choking" — were perpetrated by males acting alone and did not involve the use of weapons or result in injury. The exception to this statistic were incidents of spousal violence, where about half of Aboriginal female victims reported being injured. The public statistics might be much higher than this study found because most violent incidents against Aboriginal women are not brought to the attention of police or otherwise formally reported to any other type of victim services. Indeed, 98 percent of Aboriginal women interviewed in this study stated that they chose not to go to the police, but instead chose to confide in a friend or family member.[43]

ABORIGINAL & FIRST NATIONS GANGS

At the outset, it is important to understand that the vast majority of First Nations people are peaceful and law-abiding. Young people, like most Canadian young people, are keen and eager to better themselves as best their circumstances allow. For the most part they shun the criminals in their midst and stand apart from the gangs. The good news is that "ordinary Canadians" need not fear violence from the majority of Aboriginal people. Canadians and First Nations especially, however, do need to confront the minority in the community who belong to and/or support the several First Nations gangs now established in various reserves and in many Canadian cities and municipalities off-reserve.

A host of interconnected community factors almost inevitably "… make Aboriginal youth vulnerable to youth gang recruitment and put them at risk of incarceration [in jails and prisons], which has been described as a 'training ground' for gangs." Chief among these so-called "root causes" are social and economic instability of families; a lack of reliable access to individual and family basic needs; and lack of community resources — medical, educational, and security — to meet the basic requirements of the population. Many of these so-called root causes are, however, themselves the product of something else: the Residential School System of the last century, which gave rise to the "… destruction of families, and which, in turn, gave rise to increased Aboriginal youth mental concerns, homelessness, attachment disorders, and juvenile criminality, as well as low educational attainment, poverty, and suicide."[44] The majority of First Nations young people on-reserve live in the traumatizing environment that is the product of that system — the fertile ground in which gang members are cultivated.

For those Fist Nations living off-reserve, the situation is different. Most Canadians would be surprised to learn that from an economic and a social perspective First Nations people off-reserve fare much better living those than on-reserve — a truth that is especially true for women working in conventional, legitimate jobs and for members of stable First Nations families. However, the increased tendency of unaccompanied young people to drift away from reserves is fast building a growing First Nations "in-need" cohort in cities and towns across Canada. This is especially true in the Prairie provinces.[45] This group is particularly vulnerable to gang recruitment and the temptation of criminal activity. It is inevitable, therefore, that as the young population grows ever more rapidly over the next decades, Aboriginal criminal and gang-related problems will increase on and off-reserve — inevitable unless some effective federal, provincial, and First Nations co-operative strategy is launched in the near future to forestall this otherwise certain social disaster.

According to Mark Totten, a noted scholar of Aboriginal gangs:

> There is an epidemic of Aboriginal youth gang violence in Canada today. The rate at which Aboriginal young gang members are killing each other and committing suicide far exceeds levels of such extreme violence in any other group in Canada, perhaps in the world. If we fail to implement evidence-based crime prevention models now, things will get much worse very shortly. The Aboriginal birth rate is rapidly increasing — the child and youth population in many cities and rural areas will double within the next decade. We cannot assume that gang activity is a "reserve problem." It is not out of our sight nor out of our minds, because Aboriginals are rapidly exiting the reserves.[46]

"Aboriginal youth gangs are visible groups that come together for profit-driven criminal activity and severe violence."[47] In 2010, Canadian police forces assumed that the "[g]angs' stock-in-trade included drug distribution, prostitution [of mostly Aboriginal women], and theft."[48] Increasingly, however, the illegal production of and trade in "cheap" tobacco and cigarettes has become the chief source of gang funds; these funds that are "re-invested" in drugs, firearms, and human smuggling.

Controlling and policing the trade in the First Nations is complicated by various treaty interpretations and "jurisdictional challenges." For example, the Akwesasne Mohawk territory, a significant conduit for national and international tobacco, arms, and drug smuggling, straddles the Ontario/ Quebec and the Canada/United States borders. The RCMP national security intelligence sources in 2013 identified thirty-five specific, organized crime groups in Ontario and Quebec that take advantage of these legal uncertainties to conduct illegal cross-border operations.[49]

Even where policing and prosecution are successful, the continued incarceration of Aboriginal gang members has become, according to some police officials, another escalating problem. "Street gangs have long wreaked havoc inside Canada's male prison system … from running drugs and starting riots to targeting enemies behind bars." Prisons are also near perfect recruitment centres. "Inmates who are not members of a gang when they enter jail often are [members] by the time they are released."[50] Young people on release from prison most often return to or migrate into criminal gangs and other harmful (to themselves and society) anti-social situations simply because gangs provide them with companions, material support, and, sadly, "a meaning for being."

Officials managing youth crime and rehabilitation today face another "… emerging challenge … how to keep gang problems out of jails as a record number of women are arrested for violent crimes." Since 2001, "the number of Aboriginal women going to prison has grown by a stunning 90 percent."[51] Many of these inmates have strong ties to First Nations gangs, as in the male prisons. Once committed to prison, they act as recruiters and enforcers and as intelligence agents for gang leaders both in the all-male institutions and on the outside. Like their male counterparts, these women are making Canadian prisons increasingly dangerous places. Donald Head, commissioner of Correctional Service Canada, made this point in a rather understated comment in 2012: "There's no question that, overall, the [female] gang issue is becoming more challenging for us."[52]

The Correctional Investigator of Canada (the ombudsman for federal offenders) noted in his 2013 "Backgrounder" report concerning Aboriginal offenders that although the Aboriginal population in Canada is only about 4 percent of the national population, Aboriginals represent 23.2 percent of incarcerated Canadians in federal institutions. Moreover, he reported, "[I]n 2010–2011, Canada's overall incarceration rate was 140/100,000 adults ... a rate 10 times higher than the incarceration rate for non-Aboriginals." He noted also that "[A]boriginal offenders are much more likely than others to have their parole revoked, less likely to be granted day or full parole, most often released on statutory release or held until warrant expiry date." Aboriginal offenders were also most likely to be returned to custody after release and twice as likely to be affiliated with Aboriginal gangs.[53]

Young Aboriginal people fill Canada's jails and prisons. In 2011, Aboriginal female youth comprised 33.6 percent of all female youth in the federal correctional system. Aboriginal male youth made up 24 percent of all male youth in the correctional system.[54] The true dimensions of the incarceration of Aboriginal people in Canada can be seen only when the provincial and territorial statistics are added to the federal statistics.[55] In 2010/2011, an estimated 27 percent of all adult prisoners in provincial and territorial custody were Aboriginal and an astonishing 41 percent of all female prisoners were Aboriginal.[56]

One must assume that these people were incarcerated for good and legal reasons. Nevertheless, it is not the immediate causes for their detention that should give us pause, but rather the underlying and continuing externalities, the underlying factors, that put them in situations that arguably led them to a clash with Canada's legal system and then to imprisonment.

Most experience observers cite "substance abuse, inter-generational abuse and residential schools, low levels of education, employment, and income, substandard housing and health care" as significant "offending circumstances" that inevitably place — mostly young — Native men and women on a road to jail or prison. Other studies include "criminal history, pro-criminal associated and pro-criminal attitudes" as major contributing factors.

Certainly, criminals deserve to be punished. The better approach, however, would be to tackle the offending circum-stances that in many cases lead to criminal association and criminal behaviour. Failure to redress the underlying causes of anti-social behaviour will simply ensure that the treadmill from the reserve to city streets to gangs and thence to prison will con-tinue to run without end. Activating such a national policy has little to do with charity; rather, it would be but the first step in mending our fractured society so as to secure our future together.

THE LAW IN CANADA AND THE FIRST NATIONS

It's important for all Canadians to understand that the discus-sion and commentary presented in this chapter is the reality of Aboriginals in Canada. The First Nations people, and especially those living on-reserve, live in circumstances devised for them and administered by non-Aboriginal legislators and enforced in the main by non-Aboriginal officials, police, and courts. Is it any wonder that most First Nations people believe that the non-Aboriginal community designed its social and legal structure and policies solely to assure its own well-being and to exclude the Native people from Canada's riches?

Even if one were to assume that the social, legal, and political structures in Canada were fair and that the circumstances of First Nations life in Canada was the result of their own decisions and that their people locked up in Canada's jails and prisons where put there after a just trial, only the most hardhearted among us would not admit that Canada today is a fractured nation.

The fractures are growing and widening. The First Nations people are frustrated and most are openly hostile to Canada's domination of their lives and society and are demanding fundamental changes to their place in Canada. Yet, many Canadians respond to demands for fairness and change with indifference and cynicism and complex legal challenges. Heedless of Lincoln's warning Canadians seem to believe that their divided house will remain safe and secure without any renovations.

The reality for non-Aboriginal Canadians is that opportunities to heal peacefully the social, legal, and ethical fractures developing between our communities are slipping away. If the generally negative attitudes voiced by each side against the other continue, then tomorrow in their shared future Aboriginal and non-Aboriginal children will have to live with the possibility — indeed, the inevitability — of a civil confrontation, a possibility their parents seemed so willing to ignore today.[57]

4

CONFLICTS AMONGST THE PEOPLE

"Civil war is the most prevalent form of large-scale violence and is massively destructive to life, society, and the economy."

— *Paul Collier[1]*

Communal strife or *civil war*, ironic as the term may be, is arguably the most destructive and yet the most common form of warfare in human history. People have been beating and murdering their neighbours and "those others" for centuries, sometimes in small battles of the commons and often in widespread, continual wars between clans and dynasties. In the Middle Ages in Europe, royal families fought each other routinely. They burnt down villages and towns, besieged cities, and plundered the countryside for years at a time. Poor people, "soldiers of the king," robbed, raped, and ruined other poor people at the command of their sovereigns. These most uncivil wars were not civil wars as we may think of them today, however; they were simply the customary wars waged in the circumstances of the time. Indeed, in some parts of the world, for instance in many regions of Africa and the Middle East, this style of warfare is fought even today.

The *idea* and literature of civil warfare originated more or less coincidentally with the development of the *idea* and establishment of the nation-state. That is to say, as states evolved, warfare came to be seen as a political activity conducted by and under the authority of recognized states' governments against other recognized states' governments. Eventually, it was the idea and conduct of such international conflicts that differentiated civil wars as a particular form of warfare in both theory and literature.

Unfortunately, since the end of the Second World War, civil warfare has become the pre-eminent form of military action. In communities large and small, many such wars have been fought since then, resulting in the killing of millions of people and the destruction of vast amounts of property — all to decide who will command the spoils.

The civil wars of the early twenty-first century, while still having the appearance of battles between a government, legitimate or otherwise, and a rival faction looking to replace the sitting government, have evolved — some might say devolved — into a new form reminiscent of the violent civil wars of the thirteenth century. Rather than being wars between the political factions of a state, they are more often today, as British general Sir Rupert Smith defined them, "wars amongst the people." Many governments — think of the Balkans in the 1990s, and Libya, or Syria, or Ukraine today — face, in Smith's words, a new paradigm, a new reality "… in which the people in the streets and houses and fields — all the people, anywhere — are the battle-field. Military engagements can take place anywhere, with civilians around, against civilians, in defence of civilians. Civilians are the targets, [the] objectives to be won, as much as an opposing force."[2]

While scholars might generally define the civil wars of our age as "... large scale organized violence ... [involving] at least one private, non-governmental actor,"[3] this generalization doesn't take anyone interested very far toward understanding the *causation*, generally or specifically, of these modern conflicts. Greater precision is difficult to attain, however, as the characteristics, dynamics, and trajectory of most types of civil war, such as a modern insurgencies, are exceedingly complex. Scott Moor captures well the difficulties the academic world (to say nothing of most military establishments) has in finding a practical and agreed guide in the common term, *insurgency*:

> The term *insurgency* conjures often widely disparate interpretations, suffering at the hands of both experts and pundits. Commonly accepted meanings remain elusive, with predictable conceptual confusion. *Insurgency* continues to be used interchangeably, and imprecisely, with *irregular warfare, unconventional warfare, revolutionary warfare, guerrilla warfare* and even *terrorism*. *Insurgents*, similarly, have been called *guerrillas, terrorists, revolutionaries, extremists,* and *irregulars*. The interchangeability of terms is understandable, given the diverse nature and

adaptability of those who wage insurgency and the overlapping traits of these types of conflicts. Insurgents employ guerrilla and terrorist tactics, espouse revolutionary and radical causes, pose asymmetric threats to modern conventional forces, operate on the legal and moral margins of societies, and blur distinctions between civilians and combatants. The very use of the term *insurgency* creates legal confusion, as it infers [*sic*] a level of legitimacy that can pose political problems to ruling governments and counterinsurgent forces. All this adds up to a level of conceptual uncertainty clouding our understanding of [a particular] strategic problem.[4]

This study of Canada and the First Nations is not a lecture on these terminological difficulties, nor is it an attempt to label present or future actions stemming from First Nations conflicts with government as acts of rebellion, or revolution, or insurgency, except in very general ways. To do so would require a lengthy theoretical dissertation and that is not the intent of this work. Besides, the practical reality is that modern civil wars amongst the people, as General Smith suggests, are likely to be prolonged, perhaps on-again-off again, confrontations (see "the troubles" in Ireland of this and the last century), which may, from time to time, have the characteristics of one or several of these broadly defined challenges to governments. Beware also: governments, people in the street, and insurgents all have an interest in defining their causes and actions as worthy and legitimate. Thus, those fighting the government frequently refer to those running the state as "dictators" and to themselves as "freedom fighters," while governments typically label their opponents as "criminals" and "terrorists." So, in any discussion of civil strife and those involved in incidents of it, it is important to keep in mind the loaded values inherent in the terminology used. This is the case, too, in the present discussion.

Terminological issues aside, it is important before describing the factors that might ignite a First Nations' insurrection to highlight the social importance and legitimacy of civil protests in a democratic state such as Canada. Protests might involve a single citizen, placard on a stick held high, marching back and forth on Parliament hill. They might involve hundreds of citizens protesting some government policy or action, such as, for instance, multitudes did during the June 2010 so-called G8 meetings in Toronto. The First Nations' "Idle No More" (INM) movement is a nascent, legitimate civil protest generally characterized by peaceful First Nations' attempts to bring their concerns and demands to the attentions of Canadians.

Even in cases where, for whatever reason, a protest or demonstration *spontaneously* "gets out of hand," it is important to consider that the overwhelming majority of such situations are routine law and order matters requiring only an appropriate, reasonable, and lawful intervention by police services. The border between such protests and a hostile civil incident is often difficult to find in the midst of an excited crowd and the re-establishing of order, as during the so-called Oka Crisis of 1990. Even in extraordinary circumstances, such as the

Oka Crisis, such incidents can usually be resolved with some bargaining and compromise among all the parties involved — unless, of course, the strongest party decides it doesn't need to bargain. When that decision is taken the ordinary avenues for negotiation disappear and more extreme possibilities — uprisings, for example — appear.

Suggesting the possibility of a First Nations uprising takes one into sensitive territory. First, the choice of a term to describe a First Nations' strategy meant to propel and accelerate their people's interests can, as Scott Moore suggests, create conceptual and rhetorical confusion and, perhaps, immobilize any rational responses to threats even before any fundamental and substantive issues are placed on the table.[5] Notwithstanding the risk of taking the conversation down this track, it is a necessary trip.

If anticipating seriously the possibility of some type of civil unrest involving First Nations and the Canadian state, it is necessary at the outset to develop a plausible scenario for such a situation. Fortunately, there is credible research focused on the factors that spark such uprisings and on how they might develop that can guide us. From this research of cause and effects it is possible to estimate the likelihood of a First Nations insurgency and then propose positive deterrent measures and policies to forestall the possibility of an uprising occurring at all.

So, why do insurgencies occur? How might a First Nations insurgency unfold? What could Canada, in co-operation with First Nations leaders, do to deter such an insurgency from becoming the story of Canada's future? This chapter reviews the two generally accepted academic responses to the first question of causation: "greed and grievances" and "feasibility." Subsequent chapters will build on these theoretical explanations and set out some concepts and possible policy frameworks that might lead to deterring an insurgency well before some error or miscalculation ignites a Canadian national tragedy.

CLASSIC THEORIES ON THE ORIGINS OF INSURGENCIES

The search for the causes of and cures for civil wars has engaged scores of scholars over many years. Early research focused principally on the individual and the state. Generally, studies from this starting point have, over the last thirty years or so, theorized that the main stimulus motivating individuals to act together and challenge governments are "greed and grievances" or some combination of the two motives.

The theoretical assumption is that a "root cause" of civil conflicts is greed: the insurgent wishes to seize the power of the state in order to reap the benefits derived from control of the nation's treasury, especially, the opportunity to collect "taxes" and to control the state's valuable natural resources. Insurgent governments or factions in these types of regimes rarely have much interest in governing a state or region, except when doing so enhances the insurgent leader's welfare. Insurgencies motivated by greed may attract internal or external forces. Such forces may be composed and supported by homogeneous paramilitary ethnic groups, mixed ethnic forces, armed forces from neighbouring states, mercenaries, or other forces — all will be more or less intent on capturing control of a state's wealth.

In Canada, a form of First Nations greed/economic opportunities insurgency is evident, at least from the point of view of the federal government, police, and customs officials, in the widespread smuggling of tobacco, drugs, guns, and other contraband in and through reserves, especially on the Canada-United States border. Such activities in turn breed criminal gangs on-reserve and disadvantage residences and their security. From the perspective of some First Nations leaders, however, these businesses are legal economic entities derived from traditional trading practices of the many First Nations in Canada and the United States. At present, these types of activities and Canadian attempts to stop them have been treated more or less as common customs violations. Beneath the surface they are, in fact, a First Nations challenge to Canada's sovereignty and a Canadian challenge to First Nations' sovereignty. If left unresolved, then hostilities seem all but certain.

The *grievance* root cause or causation thesis is constructed on the premise that a deeply established major grievance or a catalogue of persistent lesser grievances resident in a significant part of a community and attributed to the attitudes and policies of the dominant society or government will provide the fuel for an uprising by the aggrieved community against the government deemed responsible for their grievances. Typically, such grievances arise when the ruling regime deprives an identified "inferior" community of basic material goods, such as, for instance, food, shelter, employment, or a fair share of the nation's riches and any means of acquiring them. As well as suffering economically, this underclass, from their perspective, will often see themselves as suffering from social, religious, and racial discrimination.

Their political rights will likely be restricted in some respect, thus denying that population any possibility to influence, let alone change, the position they occupy in that society.

These situations can ignite two types of violent civil reactions. First, as theory suggests, an insurgency may develop when the disadvantaged segment of society attempts, through violence, or even mostly peaceful means, to redress their (perceived) inferior situation by displacing the incumbent regime and, thus, seizing the social/political advantages for themselves. On the other hand, governments may sense the approaching danger and respond, not with reforms, but with armed force and more restrictive social/political counter-measures. One can see these sorts of actions and counter-actions on most every television network news broadcast. In the past few years, the drama has been played out (and continues to play out) in, for example, Libya, Syria, and Rwanda. In the spring of 2014, the cameras shifted to the Crimea and to Eastern Ukraine.

In Canada, First Nations grievances have a long history, beginning generally when the so-called "settlers" began to move into the northern regions of Ontario and, especially, into the Western territories in what is now Manitoba, Saskatchewan, and Alberta. The earlier, relatively quiet arrival and limited expansion of French and, later, the English settlers and traders provided in some ways, in the fur trade industries for example, material benefits to the Native population.

During the first half of the eighteen century, however, "…the First Nations in Western Canada underwent profound demographic and territorial changes" that altered, irretrievably, the Native culture and welfare in Canada.

The communities of the Plains Indians and the Woodlands populations across most of the northwestern regions were devastated by diseases that spread rapidly from community to community. These plagues of small pox, tuberculosis, measles, and other highly contagious epidemics wiped out entire families and, in some cases, whole villages. Starvation overtook the sick, weak, and the young. The political structure of the First Nations generally collapsed, as did their leadership, and by 1870, with the annexation of the Northwest by the Dominion of Canada, the Native community was changed forever. These facts are not simply part of a distant history; rather, they are the foundation for the grievances the First Nations present to Canada today.[6]

Most of this legacy of sorrow is remembered in indigenous stories handed down from one generation to the next. The failure of successive Canadian governments to honour, decade after decade, the treaties and obligations made or accepted from the Crown is not merely a historical fact; it is today's reality and the source of most Aboriginal grievances confronting Canadians in 2014. It is the context for all of the interactions between Natives and non-Natives in Canada today.

It was part of the background when, in July 1990, a plan by the village of Oka, Quebec, to build a golf course on land claimed by the Kanesatake First Nation exploded into a violent, armed insurrection. A police officer was killed and the federal government eventually (under the terms of the Aid of the Civil Powers legislation in place at the time) acquiesced to the province's demand for the assistance of the Canadian Armed Forces.[7] The confrontation continued for several weeks and ended more-or-less peacefully after weeks of threats from both sides, although not before several ugly scenes of non-Native civilians attacking unarmed Native women and children.

It was part of the background in August 1995, when the RCMP began a standoff at Gustafsen Lake, British Columbia, prompted by a dispute over "private property" claimed by local ranchers and the rights to the "unceded" land made by Shuswap First Nation. The armed confrontation eventually resulted in an exchange of gunfire between the warriors — "the occupiers" — and the police, and the disabling of a Native vehicle by explosive devices. After thirty days and the deployment of some four hundred police officers and members of the Canadian Armed Forces, the incident ended as a draw.

On September 4, 1995, Chippewas of Kettle Point and Stoney Point First Nations occupied Ipperwash Provincial Park, land that had belonged to these First Nations long before the British arrived in what is now Ontario. The announced intent of the Chippewas' peaceful occupation was to reinforce their claims to the land. Two days later, an occupier, Dudley George, was killed during a confrontation between the Aboriginal occupiers and the Ontario Provincial Police. The final public inquiry into the events at Ipperwash revealed serious failures on the part of the police. But in fairness to the police officers at the scene, the inquiry emphasized that the provincial government, and particularly the premier, were adamant that the occupiers be removed from the site and that no negotiations were to be considered.[8] No insurrection, properly speaking, had been contemplated by the Native demonstrators when they began their protest. The government's refusal to negotiate, however, and its hard line position created a situation in which violence was the almost inevitable outcome.

Another major, life-threatening First Nations-Canadian land confrontation occurred at Caledonia, Ontario. In February 2006, a small party of members from the Six Nations reserve began a violent campaign aimed at chasing developers from an off-reserve residential building site, Douglas Creek Estates, which the demonstrators claimed was being constructed on their land. The Native protesters harassed citizens who were not on the reserve, vandalized property, set fire to a bridge, and hijacked a police car, among other violent acts.[9]

In her detailed report on the Caledonia confrontation, Christie Blatchford drew particular attention to the OPP's reluctance to enforce the laws and to arrest the aggressive First Nations people. She described reports that confirmed why the commissioner of the OPP, Julian Fantino, was reluctant to act against the law-breaking Natives. Outside observers need to see the "bigger picture" he said, and explained: "Caledonia is not an isolated stand-alone issue. Caledonia is connected with all these other First Nations issues not only across the province, but country-wide. Everyone's watching what goes on in Caledonia and one misstep in Caledonia will result in a flare-up right across the country of conflicts and confrontation."[10]

The commissioner may have been right in that particular situation, but he may have simply surrendered to an imagined threat and the false idea that First Nations across Canada are closely united, even though at the time there was no credible evidence that they were. Nevertheless, his excuse for not acting haunts Canadian politicians and government officials every time a "First Nations incident" arises.

As natural resource exploration and extraction continues in new areas of the country, some of which are claimed by

First Nations, new land claims–based grievances arise and more protests are launched. In October 2013, for instance, Houston-based Southwestern Energy Company's (SWN) exploratory shale gas fracking development in New Brunswick was halted by violent members of the Elsipogtog First Nations. Over several days, the RCMP detachment sent to the area to enforce a court injunction and to restore order was attacked by citizens who blockaded roads, threw Molotov cocktails at police officers, and destroyed police vehicles. In the ensuing melee, dozens of people were arrested. Spontaneous solidarity protests erupted in Vancouver, Winnipeg, Victoria, Toronto, Hamilton, and Montreal. In Vancouver, supporting "activists" were able to shut down the seaport for an hour until a police assault dispersed them. In December, SWN completed its work and left the province, but with no clear indication that the company would return.[11]

There are, of course, several successful and co-operative First Nations-industry enterprises developing in many Canadian provinces and territories. For example, the Alberta-based Fort McKay Group of Companies is owned by the Fort McKay First Nations and includes nine joint ventures "looking at $600 million to $700 million in revenues a year." Other First Nations in Alberta and other regions rich in natural resources are looking for partnership opportunities as well. These successes are built on trust and transparency, allowing "First Nations … to make up their own minds" on resource development.[12] The matter, however, is very unsettled, and threats against other projects such as the Northern Gateway pipeline and other Alberta-British Columbia resource-based ventures continue.

The confrontations between Canada and the First Nations are not only motivated by disputes over control of natural resources; they are driven also by a wide array of social grievances. For example, the crisis created by the federal government's 2014 First Nations Education Act and the rejection of that act by some, but not all, First Nations is an example of a government attempt to address a social grievance that became itself the source of a social grievance. Citing a failure to consult when drafting the legislation, one group of First Nations leaders reacted to the government initiative with an immediate and hostile threat to "… shutdown Canada's economy from coast to coast."[13]

This type of response is becoming increasingly prevalent. In fact, the history of confrontations between the First Nations and Canadian governments is a story of accumulating grievances and a growing inclination for leaders to use or threaten to use violent means to compel governments to accommodate the First Nations interests and objectives as the First Nations define them. According to the sophisticated research supporting the greed and grievances theories of insurgencies, it is the perception of very longstanding "abuses" that provides the combustible material that ignite rebellions or widespread insurrections. There is, however, a need here for caution. What one side considers a grievance may not be deemed so by the other side in a dispute, and, therefore, it is not always appropriate to assume that every grievance is in fact free of self-interest and thus reasonable and worthy of uncritical redress.[14]

Furthermore, the theory that greed and/or grievances serve as the causes of civil unrest is not universally supported. Indeed, in recent years this theory has been openly challenged by other more convincing and useful theories that seek to explain why insurgencies occur and how they might be prevented. As

Oxford University researcher Paul Collier explains, the difficulty and criticism of the grievance theory is that its "… argument that violence will *inevitably* occur unless such grievances are addressed seems … counter-productive as it becomes subject to hijacking by advocacy groups with their own pet agendas. [This] root cause method of explanation is inextricably linked to the notion that the cause of rebellion is some objective grievance. But this is incorrect."[15]

In other words, just because a rebellious intervention appears to be motivated by a justifiable grievance, that grievance should not be taken as the causation for the rebellion without reference to other factors that might have ignited it and influenced its success or failure. New research also illustrates that a successful insurgency does not assure that the initiating grievance will be redressed completely, if at all. It may persist because it might serve the interests of the new faction in command much as it did the ousted regime. This possibility is so commonly expected by diplomats and scholars of international affairs that when a former subservient ethnic community replaces peacefully the absolute powers of a former oppressive government without much obvious retribution, as Nelson Mandela's African National Congress government did in 1991, it is cheered and admired.[16]

The continuing criticism of the greed and grievance theory is that it has no answer to the question: Why do insurgents not occur even in the face of serious and persistent grievances? If, therefore, the greed and grievance thesis is fatally flawed, or, at best, an unreliable base for predicting and deterring insurrections, then what will provide a more consistent theoretical framework to explain the occurrences of insurgencies and a guide to anticipating and preventing them?

THE FEASIBILITY HYPOTHESIS

The feasibility hypothesis as an explanation for the occurrence of civil conflict is attributed in the main to Paul Collier and his colleagues, who are, notably, economists and not political scientists. Collier's team decided that the study of civil conflict was "particularly well-suited to statistical analysis."[17] Their research objective was to allow researchers to consider the causes of civil conflict within a rigorous standard model without reference to any particular conflict but across scores of national examples in particular circumstances.

The Oxford statistical analysis of civil conflicts was constructed on the evidence assembled in five-year periods from 1965 to 2004 from some eighty-four conflicts. It does not discount entirely motivation as having an influence on these events. However, their data led to the postulation that "[I]nstead of the circumstances which generate a rebellion being distinctive in terms of motivation, they might be distinctive in the sheer financial and military feasibility of rebellion."[18] The team argue that motivation is essentially and practically *indeterminate* and reflects, initially at least, "…the preferences of the social entrepreneur" [or revolutionary leader — a Mao Zedong or Castro, for example] who first convinces people to support his personally defined motives or political agenda.[19]

Collier sets aside the greed and grievance theory and offers instead the feasibility hypothesis: "Factors that are important for the financial and military feasibility of rebellion but are unimportant to motivation decisively increase the risk of civil war."[20] Therefore, it follows that the prevention and/or suppression of insurgencies and rebellions requires determined efforts directed at making such uprisings less feasible — for example, by removing or remedying those factors that make an insurgency feasible in the first instance.

THE DETERMINANTS OF FEASIBILITY

Collier's team's impressive and detailed research concludes that feasibility is contingent on five major and related determinants summarized here.[21]

- **Social fractionalization:** The division of a society by ethnic and religious cleavages significantly increases risk. In its modelling, Collier's team doubled the fractionalization in its model nation from 18 percent to 36 percent, raising the risk of conflict from 4.6 percent to 6.67 percent. Social cleavages may incite armed or unarmed efforts by the minority to change its social/political circumstances. On the other hand, such demands for change might intensify the majority's resistance, possibly producing even violent resistance, to any change at all.[22]
- **The proportion of males 15–29 YOA in the population:** "Doubling the proportion of the population in this category increases the risk of conflict from 4.6 to 19.7 percent."[23]
- **The state's topography:** The researchers used the proxies, "mountainous or flat," to represent the idea that terrain can produce a potentially large effect on feasibility. For example, in their model they assume that "… were Nepal flat the risk of civil war would

be 3.5 percent" Given however the reality that "…
67.4 percent [of Nepal] is mountainous, its risk was
7 percent." The general conclusion is that "mountainous" (i.e. difficult) terrain is harder to defend
than "flat" terrain and thus a rebellion is more
feasible in difficult terrain, or — just to complete
the thought — rebel operations are more or less
infeasible in open, flat terrain.[24]

- **The proportion of primary commodity exports
  (i.e., natural resources) in GDP:** This factor is
  particularly significant when it coincides with
  the third factor. In Collier's model, "the risk of
  dependence upon primary commodity exports
  [and thus of conflict] is at its peak when exports
  constitute 25 percent of GDP." Two measures
  intensify the primary resources/GDP risk factor.
  First, risk increases exponentially as the distance
  between the sources of natural resources and
  economic goods and their foreign or domestic
  markets increases. Second, risk increases yet again
  where transportation systems are long and cross
  "mountainous terrain" and where alternative routes
  are limited or unavailable. These circumstances
  make defence complex and expensive (i.e., in the
  number of security forces required) while making
  offence relatively easy and inexpensive. In such
  circumstances, vulnerability increases for one side
  and feasibility increases for the other.[25]

- **Increased certainty of a credible security guarantee:** A guaranteed credible security force makes civil
  war more dangerous for insurgents and thus less

feasible. In Collier's research, African states where a guarantee (such as protection from a credible national or an international armed force, e.g. the United Nations) existed "faced a risk of 2.6 percent," compared with "a civil war risk of 8.2 percent" in states without such a guarantee.[26]

These determinants, especially in combination and where deeply established in an ethnic community, make states more or less vulnerable. Vulnerability in turn makes insurgencies more or less feasible. As Collier concludes, "where a rebellion is feasible it will occur."[27]

The theory's value lies in its political/policy utility: If insurgencies are to be avoided or supressed, then one or all of the determinants must be redressed in ways that reduce a state's vulnerability to insurgency. The policy therapy is disarmingly simple: "if the incidences of civil war are to be reduced ... [they] will need to be made more difficult [to instigate]."[28]

To summarize: the feasibility hypothesis does not dismiss entirely from the study of civil conflict motives such as greed and grievances. Indeed, it is difficult to imagine how a provocateur, no matter how charming and earnest, could inspire a cadre to launch a motiveless uprising. The theory does, however, argue: "In territory in which rebellion is difficult, the risk of war in any five-year period is only 0.3 percent. In other words, rebellion does not occur because it is infeasible. In a territory in which there are few impediments to rebellion, the risk that a civil war will erupt somewhere in the territory is an astonishing 99.8 percent." That is to say, it is the strength of the "determinants" outlined here and not motives alone that convince — perhaps, inspire — people to launch an insurgency. Whether that insurgency will succeed, even if it were entirely feasible, is another matter entirely.

In the following chapters, these "determinants of feasibility" will be examined in a Canada-First Nations context and from that examination an assessment can be made of the extent to which Canada may be vulnerable to a First Nations confrontation.

5

CANADA: THE VULNERABLE NATION

"Canada's economic security derived from its abundant natural resources makes Canada intrinsically insecure."[1]

The privileged — the aristocrats in the court of Louis XVI of France, or in the Romanov court in Russia; the English landlords of Ireland; the nineteenth century landed gentry of America's "Deep South"; or the assorted tyrants of today — always assume that they are without question masters of their own futures — until, that is, they suddenly discover that they are not. Likewise, a state may be insecure for a very long time without necessarily noticing it is so. Most citizens of such states tend to see their futures, though they might perhaps be unsettled from time to time by the vagaries of bothersome misfortunes, as an unending repetition of their current fortunate circumstances. This state of being seems especially so for generations who have never, or only fleetingly, experienced a widespread civil emergency or a prolonged international conflict that suddenly compromises nearly every political and social aspect of their lives.

Canada, in 2014, is such a nation. How peculiar, then, it must appear to many Canadians to suggest to them that their never-endingly prosperous world might someday be threatened by a First Nations uprising — propelled by a people who, to the majority of Canadians, don't matter.

Of course, as we have noted in preceding chapters, widespread grievances, such as those of the Aboriginals of Canada, may generate profound hostilities towards a government or regime, but rebellions ignited by such motives, absent the requisite characteristics that make them feasible, rarely succeed. The many disastrous, blood-soaked failures of such rebellions in the Soviet Union's Cold War colonies in Eastern Europe are proof enough of that reality. These failed rebellions convinced most Poles, Czechs, Hungarians, and other captives that attempting to overthrow their Soviet masters was simply not feasible, no matter how compelling their grievances. Canada's Native people too have experienced the pain of failed rebellions. The spectacular failure of Louis Riel's Northwest Rebellion of 1885 resulted in the complete defeat of the Métis-Indian force and Riel's execution, and ended also armed hostilities between Aboriginal people and the Canadian government for a time.

IF THE FEASIBILITY HYPOTHESIS FITS, WEAR IT

Moving a hypothesis from its sheltered existence as an abstract idea into the messy realities of current affairs is a challenge, but a manageable challenge.[2] This chapter begins with the assumption that the feasibility hypothesis — *Where a rebellion is feasible it will occur* — is sufficiently robust and credible to serve as a vehicle to investigate the feasibility of a serious confrontation between Canadian and First Nations communities somewhere in the future. Based on that assumption, it is possible to explore, in a practical Canadian context, the theoretical "determinants" at the centre of the hypothesis. Then, based on the observations stemming from those explorations, to draw a conclusion as to whether or not a First Nations insurgency is feasible. Once such a determination is made, then, according to the hypothesis, the conclusion is clear: if it is feasible, then such an insurgency will occur.

The feasibility hypothesis should interest Canadians for several reasons. Today, most of the emphasis in government-First Nations discussions and in public discourse is focused on addressing (or arguing about) Aboriginal grievances and the worry that "… if we don't get it right, we're headed for a lot of trouble." However, "getting it right," fixing the grievances (even if we, unrealistically, assume that new grievances will not arise), will not avert a domestic confrontation if the causation is not grievances, but feasibility.[3] The hypothesis matters also because it identifies "the determinants" that make an insurgency feasible and thus sets out for Canadians — and also for First Nations leaders — practical policy targets to reduce the feasibility of an insurgency occurring.

Let there be no doubt, avoiding a First Nations insurgency is an urgent national security necessity. Yet, it is a necessity that no government, federal or provincial, has to date been willing to acknowledge publicly, as even a possibility. Despite that, and this point is equally important, the fact that Canada's economy is significantly vulnerable to interference is a reality that many influential First Nations leaders understand all too well.

THE FEASIBILITY DETERMINANTS BROUGHT HOME

I. SOCIAL FRACTIONALIZATION (THE DIVISION OF A SOCIETY BY ETHNIC AND RELIGIOUS CLEAVAGES) INCREASES FEASIBILITY.

As noted earlier, there are approximately 850,000 First Nations people in Canada today, a number that represents 2.6 percent of the Canadian population. The First Nations population is the fastest-growing and youngest ethnic population in Canada. They are set apart from all other residents of Canada by their ancient cultures and histories and by the fact that under the Indian Act they are legally "recognized" as separate by the federal government and, therefore, unique among Canadians. By that fact alone, the people of the First Nations are fractionalized from others in Canada.

The "cleavages" are, however, demonstrated extraordinarily by other social facts. For instance, as described in Chapter Four, the First Nations as individuals and as a society within the Canadian society are unique in terms of unemployment, low standards of health, serious illness, unavailability of health services, lack of access to education at all levels, and, thus, of educational achievement. First Nations people make up the majority of the population in Canada's prisons and jails. To be a First Nations person in

Canada is to be a person who is ethnically and socially "fractionalized" from the majority Canadian society.

II. THE PROPORTION OF MALES AGED 15–19 IN THE POPULATION IS SIGNIFICANT.

The fact that the median age in the First Nations community is twenty-six is important; however, the fact that is of most relevance to the feasibility hypothesis is that an estimated 415,600 people or 48.8 percent of the First Nations population are under the age of twenty-four. Of immediate concern, in terms of the feasibility hypothesis, is a second fact: approximately 160,000 people, or 18.4 percent of the total population, are 15–24 YOA, and following this cohort is another composed of 258,000 children under the age of fourteen. By 2017, Canada could be faced with five hundred thousand First Nations people under the age of twenty-four.

Some may argue that this factor is taken out of context because First Nations youth are widely scattered across Canada in their many communities and, therefore, the fact that 48.8 percent of the total national population is under twenty-four does not in any meaningful way fit the theoretical determinant. The concern is, however, that these young people, like most of the First Nations population, are concentrated in areas critically important to Canada's resource industries and transportation infrastructure.

For instance, in 2011 the median age for First Nations people in Saskatchewan was twenty, and included 39, 275 children aged fourteen, representing 20 percent of all children in the province. Manitoba, whose First Nations population had a median age of twenty-one at the time, was home to

41,955 children, or 36.7 percent of all First Nations people in the province.[4] The majority of these people live outside of the provinces' cities and large towns, mostly residing close to the northern, resource-rich areas of the provinces, or on or near the transportation routes to and from them.

III. THE STATE'S TOPOGRAPHY [MOUNTAINOUS OR FLAT] SIGNIFICANTLY INFLUENCES THE [FEASIBILITY] OF AN INSURRECTION.

It isn't necessary to explain to Canadians the characteristics of Canada's vast, varied topography. It is, however, important for them to understand the very special consequences this topography imposes on our national economic and security policies. The main economic and security impacts of the geography "determinant," will be explained in detail later, but here it is important to simply acknowledge that Canada is divided not only into "mountainous and flat" regions (and recall that these characteristics are associated in the theoretical model with areas that are difficult or easy to maintain security), it is also geographically divided by vast forests, great plains — in the North and the West —, and enormous waterways, all of which impose considerable security challenges, even in relatively peaceful times. For Canada, the two general characteristics that "produce a potentially large effect" are the enormous territory that might need to be secured during a widespread disturbance and the great distances between these territories and the present distribution of security forces across Canada.

In today's circumstances, if even a modest Aboriginal force challenged Canada's authority outside a major metropolitan region, an adequate response might be difficult to assemble. For example, two railway corridors and the one main highway — all immensely important to Canada's economy, since they serve to connect Canada's East and West — run though the remote region between Sault Ste. Marie and the Ontario/Manitoba boundary. This region is also home to close to half (one hundred thousand) of Ontario's Native population.[5] There are no other transportation options in the region capable of replacing the railways and the highway should they, for whatever reason, become unusable.[6]

In Northwestern Ontario, peace and order are enforced by a number of small, widely separated Ontario Provincial Police (OPP) detachments. In a serious emergency, these units might be reinforced from other parts of Ontario, but that effort would be logistically difficult. More worrying is the possibility that as police resources are taken from one area to reinforce another, supporting demonstrations (i.e. rail/highway blockades) might erupt in these newly understaffed regions. The important fact to draw from all of this is that, though Canada's police forces are small and generally competent, they have very limited training or capabilities suited for internal security operations.

IV. AN INCREASED CERTAINTY OF A CREDIBLE SECURITY GUARANTEE MAKES THE RISK OF CIVIL WAR MORE DANGEROUS FOR INSURGENTS AND THUS LESS FEASIBLE.[7]

According to Collier's research, African states where a security guarantee existed (such as might be provided by a credible national or an international organization, e.g., the United Nations) "faced a [civil war] risk of 2.6 percent" compared with "a civil war risk of 8.2 percent" in states without such a guarantee.[8]

One could debate the definition of a "credible security guarantee," but in practical terms it would certainly have the following characteristics: authority to act — rules of engagement — sanctioned by a legitimate authority; a unified command structure; ability to respond in a timely manner to a demand; appropriately trained and experienced armed forces; police/military capabilities superior to those of the anticipated opposing force; and the ability to be logistically sustainable for significant periods of time.

Canadian municipal and provincial police forces have some of these characteristics, but they generally lack technical capabilities, tactical training, and sufficient numbers and logistical support to sustain a major operation over several weeks. These insufficiencies are certainly not the result of incompetence in any regard, but simply follow from the fact that Canadian police units were not created to conduct complex security operations against unified, armed opponents. The limitations of police units in such situations were apply demonstrated during the FLQ incident (October 1970), at Oka (1990) and Ipperwash (1995), and in Caledonia (2006). In any serious challenge to government authority by an individual First Nation or an alliance of First Nations groups, no one should assume that police forces alone would be considered by the members of such a rebellion as a "credible security guarantee."

The expectation that the Canadian Armed Forces (CF) are and would be the nation's "credible security guarantee" in any internal security emergency is, in most circumstances, a reasonable assumption. The armed forces exemplify the characteristics of a credible guarantee described earlier. Moreover, many of the leaders of the units of the CF that would be on the frontlines of any Aboriginal confrontation in Canada have (for at least the next decade or so) the advantage of having real operational experience, gained in Afghanistan and in other insurgency environments. Nevertheless, this assumption of credibility must be considered in light of the circumstances the armed forces would face.

For all their professional expertise, experience, and technical superiority, the CF would face serious challenges if called upon to confront anything but a limited, localized internal security incident. Canada's armed forces are small (there are at present a mere sixty-five thousand personnel, of which fewer than a third are trained combat soldiers), and this limitation is especially true of the army's combat units, which would most certainly carry responsibility for the frontline mission in any such operation.

V. THE PROPORTION OF PRIMARY COMMODITY EXPORTS (I.E., NATURAL RESOURCES) IN THE GDP IS SIGNIFICANT.

Studies of this factor have shown that the relationship between a state's security and its primary commodities exports depends not on the volume of the natural resources exports alone, but on a nation's economic dependence on such exports measured as a percentage of gross domestic product (GDP). According to Collier's analysis, "…the risk of dependence upon primary commodity exports is at its peak when exports constitute 25 percent of GDP.[9] This is obviously an issue of particular importance for Canada. In fact, the degree to which Canada is already dependent on the export of natural resources must be considered as a factor that could increase Canada's economic vulnerability and, therefore, the feasibility of a First Nations' insurgency.

The importance of natural resources to the Canadian economy and to the welfare of Canadians is remarkable. In 2012, the value of Canada's total "merchandise exports" — its metals, mining, energy, and forest products, agricultural products (grains), and other food goods — measured as a proportion of GDP was 25 percent.[10] In this basket, certain resources stand out. For example, in 2013, natural resources — energy, mining, and forestry — provided $30 billion a year in revenues to governments; employed directly and indirectly "close to 1.8 million" Canadians; and "… accounted for over 18 percent of Canada's GDP."[11] The government also reported in 2013 that Canada is "the sixth-largest exporter … of agriculture and agri-food products in the world with exports valued at $40.3 billion."[12] The industry employs 2.1 million people and accounts for 8 percent of Canada's total GDP.[13]

These industries and their employees, as well as Canada's provincial and federal governments, are hostage to a fundamental national reality: a mountain of copper ore, or gold for the taking lying in a riverbed, or a bumper crop of wheat sitting in a grain elevator in Northern Saskatchewan, have no value unless they get to market. In this vast country, getting natural resources of all types to market — in Canada, or the United States, or overseas via our ports — and importing finished products from domestic or foreign markets are both unconditionally dependant on the continuous functioning of Canada's enormous transportation infrastructure. In other words, if this infrastructure were to fail for even a few weeks, Canada's economy would likely collapse.

To damage the national transportation system to the extent that such an attack would jeopardize Canada's economy, an attacker would only have to cause the failure of a critical transportation/export system, or major parts of it, and maintain this effect long enough to significantly disrupt Canada's financial markets and its international trade. Even a suggestion that Canadian exports might become unreliable would likely result in very rough ride for the dollar in foreign markets.

GETTING THE GOODS TO MARKET

One way or another, transportation is a part of all social and economic activities [in Canada]. Transportation provides market access for natural resources, agricultural products, and manufactured goods in the same way it provides support to service industries. It also overcomes the challenges posed by topography and geography — linking communities and reducing the effects of distance that separates people from each other. These essential roles reflect transportation's intertwined and interdependent relationships with the economic engines and social fabric of our society.[14]

The national transportation infrastructure is composed of three main elements: oil and gas pipelines; heavy vehicle highways; and railways. All are vulnerable to interference. There are thousands of kilometres of oil and natural gas pipelines in Canada. Most are buried in the ground and, therefore, relatively difficult to damage. On the other hand, their above-ground, isolated pumping stations and other ancillary equipment, situated at intervals along these lines, are vulnerable and could easily be damaged.

Heavy truck transportation makes an important contribution to Canada's GDP, especially in the Southern Ontario Montreal corridor. It is responsible for the movement of a significant portion of the goods that travel into and out of the United States, and serves as a vehicle for the movement of large volumes raw materials across Canada also.[15] A serious disruption of this traffic would have a significant effect. It would not only impact Canada's import/export trade, it would also disable industries built on just-in-time delivery systems, which depend on predictable deliveries of parts and supplies to keep the systems working — Canada's automotive industries, for example.

The importance of the trucking industry and its indispensable contribution to the health of Canada's economy was demonstrated on the docks of Vancouver's ports when, in March 2014, some 1,800 truck drivers went on strike, shutting down the transportation of container traffic at the port. According to the *National Post*, "The port moves roughly $126 million worth of goods every day ..."[16] and the strike has "... had a devastating impact on business in the Lower Mainland [of] B.C. and across Canada since it began on Feb 26."[17] The reality is: no trucks, no manufacturing, and no final products or jobs.

Railway infrastructure, the heart of Canada's transportation infrastructure, is a completely different entity; however, like Canada's highways, the railways are critically important to the health of Canada's economy and vulnerable targets. The thirty "federal railways" include "three national railways" — Canadian Pacific Railway, Canadian National Railway, and Via Rail — that, with the other, smaller freight and passenger lines, carry "... 70 percent of [Canada's] freight moved on land and over seventy-three million passengers." The system, the third largest in the world, includes more than forty thousand kilometres of track, 2,900 locomotives, and employs some ten thousand people nationwide.[18]

The railways of Canada are the bulk carriers of the economy. Each year they transport millions of tonnes of natural resources to manufacturing facilities in Canada and the

United States and to East- and West-Coast ocean ports. "The commodities with the largest impact, from a tonnage perspective, are coal, iron ores and concentrates, potash, and fuel oil and crude petroleum."[19] These types of bulk cargoes cannot be moved in the volumes demanded by any system other than rail, and any long interruption in deliveries would severely disrupt exports and manufacturing businesses and the economy.

The federal government understands this fact of national life. Any disruptions, such as "capability shortages" — the lack of locomotive engines, for instance — can create major headaches for industries and governments. If these types of events are worrisome, imagine the chaos in Canada if one or both national railways were blockaded for several weeks! Such an event would of course have an enormous negative impact on Canada's economy and, therefore, the government is extremely sensitive to any possibility of threat to the railways. This sensitivity was recently demonstrated when a strike threatened the functioning of the railways, as we shall see in the next chapter. We will review the federal government's response to railway strikes and threats of such strikes for clues as to how it might react to a not-so-usual security problem in the future.

Finally, although it is not technically a "transportation facility," the vast hydroelectric systems in Canada provide a direct contribution to provincial and national economies by supplying energy to manufacturing, transportation, residential, commercial, and agricultural sectors of the economy. In 2009, for instance, these systems earned $2.4 billion in revenues from exports to the United States.[20]

The transmission infrastructure of these systems is — unfortunately for citizens and governments — almost impossible to protect, mainly because they run through hundreds of kilometres of rugged territory. It is extremely difficult for hydroelectric crews to repair failed lines and facilities in such an environment, even in ordinary circumstances, such as when bad weather brings lines down. However, for those intent on merely disabling the lines and facilities, the electrical infrastructure's size and its remoteness makes it particularly vulnerable and, thus, attractive. The security challenge faced by a threatened major energy provider in any of the provinces is enormous: for example, Hydro Québec would need to defend its 145,542 kilometres of transmission and distribution lines; Ontario Hydro would need to protect 152,451 kilometres of lines; and BC Hydro, 73,000 kilometres.[21]

Anyone who experienced the dangers and the chaos of the 1998 or the 2013 ice storms in Eastern Canada will understand the central importance of these vulnerable facilities, not only to industry, but also to Canadian households, and how difficult it is to return major systems to service once they have suffered significant damage.

The evidence supports the supposition that Canada's economy is vulnerable to major, long-term interference that would endanger not only the nation's economy, but its national security as well. Leaders in some First Nations understand this reality and the power it brings to their communities. Shawn Brant, a Mohawk living in Southeastern Ontario, is one such leader, and he describes forcefully Canada's dilemma: "The government ran its infrastructure through our land ... now it serves as an incredibly powerful tool of influence that allows us now as a society to engage the government in a dialogue, a relationship based on us having the power."[22]

On several occasions in the last few years, and twice in the winter of 2014 alone, Brant and his supporters have demonstrated his people's power by blocking the major railway corridor at Napenee, Ontario, and stopping all train movements between Montreal and Toronto at a cost of many millions of dollars to the Ontario and Canadian economies. He did this with a scruffy crew of four or five "warriors"!

FROM THEORY TO REALITY

The next chapters of this book will trace just how a First Nations insurgency might unfold in Canada. First, however, it might be helpful to bring together briefly the principle concepts of the feasibility theory of insurgency and Canada's situation and circumstances. In doing so, this work might alert citizens and leaders in both communities to the possibility that we may have together constructed, more or less unknowingly, a dangerous social-political environment for ourselves.

Fractionalized states, those divided along racial, economic, religious, and ethnic lines, are especially prone to unrest and rebellions. Canada and the First Nations, as we have already noted, is fractured by laws — predominantly by the Indian Act — and by Canada's Aboriginal polices that together unfairly place the people of the First Nations at an enormous disadvantage.

The two communities are divided as well in their demographic structures. The First Nations are significantly younger and growing rapidly, while the non–First Nations community is aging and barely growing at all. Canada's social-political policies regarding its Aboriginal population, together with, in many cases, the neglect of First Nations leaders of their own communities, are producing a young Native society that is disadvantaged and angry and prone to anti-social activities.

These young people — and especially the large number of 15–19 YOA males — provide the "warriors" that criminal gangs and rebel leaders are seeking.

Canada's topography is particularly suited to insurgent activities because it is difficult to defend and easy to attack. Canada has over many decades and at great expense constructed one of the world's most elaborate transportation systems. It is the blood and guts of our natural resources and industrial wealth and transports annually more than 20 percent of Canada's GDP. The system is, however, almost impossible to defend, as Shawn Brant and others like him have demonstrated, and invites attacks by aggrieved people who live nearby, on what is in many cases still contested land.

The security reality is that Canadian leaders over many years have almost absentmindedly placed Canada's economic welfare in the hands of thousands of people who plan to be "idle no more."

The feasibility of a First Nations insurgency in Canada could be frustrated if not entirely defeated by redressing the national factors that have made a First Nations insurgency feasible. We shall learn in the next few years whether our leaders are wise enough to develop quickly such a plan and the supporting policies that will make Canada's future secure for everyone. The following chapters sketch out the likely outcomes if they fail in this most serious duty.

6

IMAGINING A
FIRST NATIONS REBELLION

"A covert operation involving burning cars on every railway would almost be impossible to stop despite all the Canadian military and police being alerted to the potential."

— *Chief Terry Nelson, 2012*[1]

A successful rebellion requires strong leaders, who manage, in a consistent fashion, a coherent strategy, within an effective, unified organization that conducts armed operations according to an agreed upon, carefully constructed plan. There is no such structure in the First Nations community today. There is no coherent strategy; there are no clear objectives, no unified organization, and no plan. But there are in Canada in 2014 indications and warnings that the underlying support within the community to develop a unified First Nations strategy for coherent civil action is building.

Where these serious matters will take the nation, Canadians can only imagine. Asking, however, where the gathering unrest within the First Nations community might lead and then imagining just how a First Nations rebellion might unfold are prudent actions that Canadian leaders ought to consider seriously.

THE ELEMENTS FOR SUCCESS

The success of an insurgency is typically measured by the degree to which it can achieve its political objectives, meaning, in most cases, the degree to which is can usurp the power of the state or regime it is attacking. Assessing that possibility of success before an insurgency is launched requires, first, a clear understanding of the dominant characteristics of an insurgency and, second, an estimation of the "enemy's" strengths and weaknesses as compared to those of the defending force.

THE CHARACTERISTICS OF AN INSURGENCY

An insurrection is a politically motivated action involving armed forces aimed at isolating, destabilizing, and overthrowing a ruling government. In their early stages, insurgencies are not so much aimed at "winning battles" — in fact, such "victories" are often almost irrelevant. Rather, "winning the hearts and minds of the people" is the commanding aim of any successful insurgency strategy.[2] These wars amongst the people do not need the active support of all the people all of the time, but they do engage, in one way or another, most of the people some of the time.

In developed societies, the leaders of rebellions, as a general rule, are comparatively well educated, politically astute, deeply indoctrinated individuals who understand at least the basic tenets of political warfare. Combatant recruits, on the other hand, are typically young men and often women with little education, with a deep sense of loyal to clan and culture, and without much (economically) to lose and maybe something to be gained in a battle between the people and the government.

Successful insurgency forces typically live amongst the people, non-combatant civilians, and depend on them for logistical and intelligence support — for instance, the gathering of information on the movement of government forces — they (more or less willingly) provide to the insurgents' operational units. To this end, leaders of insurgencies depend very much on winning the support of a community's opinion makers — the chiefs, or religious authorities, or informal community leaders, for instance — and at least the forbearance of most of the rest of the population.

Successful insurgent campaigns usually avoid battles with regular force military units, at least initially. Acting ambitiously too early in a campaign, when insurgent units may be poorly trained and inexperienced, may lead to significant casualties, disillusionment in their ranks, and, in some cases, outright defeat. Overly aggressive operations may also provoke a government or its military commanders to launch perhaps lethal counter-insurgency operations and/or prompt retaliatory action against the civilian population that might fundamentally damage the insurgents' relations with an otherwise helpful civilian population.

Successful rebel commanders attempt to discover what the enemy holds dear and then strike there and vanish before a counter-attack arrives. Such targets might include isolated government-appointed officials, such as mayors, police chiefs, and tax collectors; and major, critical industries and their supporting infrastructure, such as railways and highway bridges and so on. Indiscriminate attacks on civilian targets, such as car-bombing in marketplaces, or the random destruction of essential public services and infrastructure important to the people and their welfare can greatly harm a rebellion and discredit its leaders and its causes and drive away sympathetic supporters.

Most "battles" that do take place are limited affairs — often part of a "war in the shadows," that is, a war that is hidden rather than out in the open. Insurgent operations tend to become bolder over time, conducted on an ever-increasing scale until they reach a point where the government side is perceived to be mortally weak and its popular support has evaporated. At this stage, an insurgency may take on the characteristics of a more typical war involving large units and relentless combat.

It is important to note that even when spontaneous protests or uprisings manage to achieve some tactical successes, an insurgency launched by a minority population rarely succeeds in changing important government policies or gains fundamental political power or prestige for the aggrieved segment of a community. Such was the case, for example, for the radical wing of the Irish Republican Army over more than twenty years of deadly attacks. The IRA and its most violent offshoot, the "Real IRA," which through most of its campaign numbered only about five hundred hardcore members, did, however, manage to keep some twenty-five thousand British soldier tied down for years.

In Canada, the so-called Idle No More (INM) movement, while momentarily interesting and colourful, has had no significant effect on Canadian-First Nations policies or on the generally negative attitudes of non-Aboriginal Canadians toward First Nations demands. A failure that some would suggest might inspire — as it did in the ranks of the IRA — the more aggressive members of such organization to turn to more damaging methods and strategies.

THE STRATEGY BACKGROUND

In its simplest form, a strategy is made up of a statement of an objective, an outline of a plan to achieve it, and an estimate of the resources required to support the plan. Without this foundation, no credible plan for action can be constructed or executed. Therefore, building the outline of an imagined First Nations strategy must first address these three essential elements.

The starting point in such an effort is to define clearly and concisely the aims of a First Nations strategy. In 1986, First Nations leaders declared in the still-valid "Charter of the Assembly of the First Nations" the fundamental political aims of the First Nations people. In that Charter the chiefs of the Assembly of First Nations confirmed their duty to maintain their peoples' freedom, language, and traditions "… given to us by the Creator [that] cannot be altered or taken away by any other nation." The chiefs declared also that the First Nations, "part of the international community," are determined "to establish conditions under which justice and respect for the obligations arising from our international treaties and from international law can be maintained." These goals, "by virtue of the recognition and respect for our [First Nations] mutual sovereign equality" form the platform from which the AFN intended to approach Canadians and Canadian governments. These same goals hold true today, and the national chiefs of the AFN and other influential leaders have reinforced these fundamental concepts many times over the years.[3]

Shawn Atleo, national chief of the AFN from 2009 until his resignation in May of 2014, was faithful to this founding charter. His central premise, enunciated in his many public remarks, was that the First Nations are in fact "nations," each enjoying a sovereign relationship with Canada and with each other. In 2013, for example, Atleo declared that Canada and the First Nations are irrevocably equal entities: "[Treaties] bind us *in a unique partnership* secured when our ancestors agreed to peacefully *co-exist* in mutual respect and to share the land and the wealth of our traditional territories."[4]

Thus, the assumed fundamental aim of a united First Nations strategy would be to embed in Canada's Constitution and in the minds of Canadians the concept that the First Nations are sovereign entities within Canada. From this base, the expectation in the First Nations community is that the benefits of sovereignty, at least as much as they already exist between Canada and the provinces, will be enshrined in Canadian laws and regulations and reflected in Canada's national policies.

Achieving this objective would require Canada (that is, the Government of Canada) to acquiesce to this status and to all the rights and privileges that would follow from it. Accepting that obligation in any meaningful way would be a very difficult political challenge for any prime minister without the willing support of non-Aboriginal Canadians. It is an unlikely that Canadians today, or even tomorrow, would grant such changes to the status quo given the public's discontent over — at times, outright hostility toward — First Nations demands.[5]

If the expectation is that Canadians would not accept the *Charter of the Assembly of the First Nations* as anything more than First Nations rhetoric, then what strategic options would be open to the First Nations?

Initially, Canadian's should expect the First Nations to continue to press their case in the courts and in the media and other public forums. At the same time, Canadians should anticipate continued public demonstrations of various kinds, aimed, one assumes, to win concessions from the federal government. An approach that then-Chief Atleo termed in 2012 "the hard way or the harder way."[6] At the time, many chiefs across the country supported Atleo's determination, some in very much stronger language that he ever did.[7]

Canadians should expect continued special pleading in public fora, perhaps on a case-by-case basis, by First Nations leaders, in concert with escalating, *mostly* peaceful public demonstrations and acts of civil disobedience across the country. To date, the small groups of Native people chanting in the streets and/or blocking municipal roads and railway lines have been a nuisance to local authorities, but they have not had much obvious effect on federal government policies. Such protests have been too small and localized, too easily within the capabilities of local police forces to control to worry governments. The government is not completely oblivious to these events, however. It appears to be keeping a hidden eye on these events and those who direct, encourage, and attend them.

Some citizens argue that the constraints that have been placed on police forces and their management of disturbances by First Nations people are testament to the government's inability to act, or as proof of "warrior power." The reality is that if given directions to restore order, as was the case in the New Brunswick/Elsipogtog First Nations 2014 "fracking" dispute, reinforced local police units can clear the streets of such demonstrations at little cost and with few casualties. Restraint in such cases is an operational choice, not a display of either police weakness or demonstrators' strength.[8]

The public resistance to First Nations pleas and hostility towards demonstrators continues to spread across Canada, and a counter-resistance movement is likely to develop further in the non-Aboriginal community if the Native demonstrations continue or, especially, if they become more aggressive. The federal government certainly continues to challenge and resist most First Nations demands; when it does give way, it does so reluctantly, in the hope that some sort of Canada/First Nations overarching peaceful relationship can be arranged without too much put on the table by them. Inevitably, such offers by the government are only met with more angry demands from Canada's various chiefs.

Why do the leaders of the First Nations persist in this type of behaviour when it seems to produce so few positive returns? One answer is that the leaders know well that they have the potential power to isolate, destabilize, and, ultimately, wreck Canada's economy. An imagined strategy suggests that they may be correct.

A FIRST NATIONS STRATEGIC ANALYSIS

Mission: To exploit the vulnerabilities of the Canadian economy to force the Canadian government to engage the First Nations in pragmatic negotiations aimed at enhancing First Nations sovereignty in Canada.

The Guiding Assumption: Canada is vulnerable to a nation-wide insurrection because its society is "fractionalized"; the First Nations male population aged 15–24 is significant; Canada's topography is difficult to defend; its "security guarantee" is weak; and it is economically dependent on commodity exports.

These classic factors contribute to Canada's economic insecurity, especially when considered as a whole. The First Nations strategic challenge is to determine how best to exploit the feasibility determinants in Canada's political and social structure in ways that best contribute to the accomplishment of the First Nations strategic mission to enhance their sovereignty.

THE OPERATIONAL FACTORS

The large First Nations population of young males can provide experienced Native leaders with a significant potential "warrior cohort" for their recruitment base.

The nearly two million First Nations people situated across Canada are an advantage to be exploited, but the fact that this population is spread so widely is also something of a disadvantage, since it makes unified operations and command coherence difficult.

The weakness of Canadian security forces, both because of numbers and because of their scattered deployments, offers a clear advantage for the First Nations, but only if a rebellion were widespread enough to prevent Canada's security forces from concentrating in a particular area.

The influence of the population/distribution factors on any mission is unpredictable, simply because circumstances — co-operation or lack thereof in the First Nations community,

unity or interoperability of police forces, government inclination (or disinclination) to use military force early against citizens, and other "human influences" — could multiply or detract from this factor's potential effects.

Three other closely related factors, however, suggest that a mission to disable Canada's economy may not be as problematic as it might at first appear: Canada's economy is unalterably dependent on "merchandise export/import trade"; that trade is largely composed of natural resources; Canada's domestic and international trade is absolutely dependant on a few major transportation facilities and infrastructures to deliver this trade to markets; and third, a significant volume of this trade must be transported over very long distances through difficult terrain along isolated road and railway networks.

These factors make Canada's international and domestic trade vulnerable to "interference" and make Canada's economy vulnerable as a result. Of these systems, the vulnerability of the national railway networks stands out.

A FIRST NATIONS OPERATIONAL CONCEPT

The operational concept to meet the aim of the First Nations strategic mission is to exploit the transportation vulnerabilities underpinning Canada's economy and thereby create the "winning conditions" that will force the Canadian government to change fundamentally its political relationship with the First Nations.

Disrupting the nation's railway transportation system would be the enabling tactical aim of the operational plan. In general outline, the operation would concentrate on disrupting railway transportation across the entire network through the use of simultaneous blockades, damage, and other interferences with railway tracks and supporting structures. There would be no intention to deliberately harm individuals or to cause damage to communities along any railway system.

The defence plan would be constructed on the following general assumptions:

- The operation is a defensive operation and would be conducted to protect the First Nations people, their rights, and their future from Canada's political leaders and their colonialist policies.
- The disruption of the nation's critical railway infrastructure would significantly and rapidly create disastrous economic consequences for Canada.
- An armed reaction by Canada against these First Nations actions would have disastrous repercussions for the government both in terms of national unity and with respect to international relations.
- Complete disruption or dislocation of the nation's railway transportation system would not be necessary to produce significant negative effects on Canada's economy, security, and social welfare. Rather, continual widespread and unpredictable minor disruptions would suffice.
- Canada's national security forces would be incapable of guarding or defending continuously the entire railway system over a prolonged period.
- The First Nations forces, on the other hand, would hold continuously the initiative to interfere and disrupt the system at times and locations of their choosing.

- The First Nations active forces would enjoy the implicit quiet support and protection of most First Nations bands and communities, whereas the federal forces would be treated as a hostile entity and be forced to act without timely and reliable intelligence sources.
- Any pre-emptive attacks against the First Nations people or their peaceful communities by the police or the CF, or by vigilantes, would be met with an immediate response in kind, as well as by the condemnation of the international community.

The operations would be directed at critical railway and highway bottlenecks across Canada, all of which share several common characteristics: they are of immediate and significant value to businesses and governments; most are located in areas distant from major national security resources and forces; and most are close to sympathetic First Nations communities. These sites include among others:

- British Columbia's road and rail systems, which pass through the mountainous approaches to Pacific Ocean ports;
- the crude oil, coal, grain, and other natural resources industries vital to the economies of Alberta, Saskatchewan, and Manitoba;
- Winnipeg's concentrated rail and road facilities, which are the critical intersection in the country's East-West transportation system because there are no Canadian controlled by-passes around this road and rail transportation hub;[9]
- Ontario contains several vulnerable bottlenecks; for

example, the road and rail systems between Montreal and Windsor and the converging road and rail systems in the Thunder Bay/Nipigon areas north of Lake Superior;

- In the east, the bridges near Montreal and Quebec City; the East-West highways north and south of the St. Lawrence River; the highway approaches into the United States; the roads and railways systems from the Maritimes to Quebec and the United States; and the vital Halifax harbour are all undefended vulnerable targets.[10]

Given these specific vulnerabilities, an imagined concept of operations for a unified First Nations campaign directed at high-volume railway lines and locomotives and their supporting communications, signalling, and other traffic controlling facilities, could be conducted in three phases.

The Warning Phase: Active operations would be preceded by a "warning period" to announce to the public the plan to interfere with railway operations nation-wide, to explain the First Nations purpose, and outline Canada's vulnerabilities. It would include periodic demonstrations on or near railway facilities intended to confirm to Canadians the unity of the people and their determination to overturn the status quo political arrangement.

The Disruptive Phase: Widespread "no-warning" disruptive operations (aimed to minimize civilian casualties) would target, for the most part, isolated railway facilities between the Maritime provinces and Quebec; the Northern Ontario/Lake Superior routes; the Prairie grain, natural resources, and oil transportation routes; and the Alberta to Vancouver/coastal British Columbia routes.

Continuous Operations Phase: Small damaging raids would be conducted with increasing frequency and intensity across Canada.

The plan would provide intervals between or during operational phases to provide opportunities for First Nations-federal government negotiations during which Canadian leaders could present to the First Nations people fundamentally new constitutional arrangement with Canada.

IS THIS IMAGINED SCENARIO CREDIBLE?

Some Canadians no doubt might argue that there would be few First Nations people willing to join in dangerous attacks on the railways, and that even if there were the will, the Native population has neither the knowledge nor the skills or the leadership to undertake such attacks. Such people usually defend their attitudes and prejudices by situating such attacks as part of a First Nations uprising involved in the most challenging full-scale battle scenarios. Such people need to understand that an effective assault on Canada's economy could be effective without the use of sophisticated skills and guns and explosives simply because the foundation of the economy is vulnerable to very simple techniques of interference — burning cars on railway tracks would suffice. So long as the railway lines are left without constant surveillance, even uncomplicated sabotage tactics would cause significant harm to the economy.

Canadians have already experienced the damaging effects of railway closures, and have seen governments' swift, extraordinary, and rapid reactions to these interruptions. In the spring of 2012, the Teamsters Union called a strike against Canadian

Pacific Railway. The impact of the strike was felt immediately across Canada as producers waited, ships sat idle in harbours, mills closed, businesses laid off workers, and foreign customers looked for products elsewhere. According to then-Federal Minister of Labour Lisa Raitt, the CP stoppage would have cost Canada more than $540 million per week if it had been allowed to continue. Even if the strike had ended abruptly, the costs were predicted to continue until CP workers were able to bring the railway back to full capacity and clear the cargo backlog. The federal government followed the situation carefully and in five days intervened and brought an end to the strike.[11]

A similar scrimmage occurred when the Teamsters Union organized their Canadian National Railway members to strike in early 2014. The government warned CN and the Teamsters that it "… would use back-to-work legislation to keep the country's biggest railway operating." An agreement was struck soon afterwards and the three thousand workers continued working.[12]

Even inconvenient weather, some say, can disrupt Canada's railway-dependent economy. Western grain farmers complained in 2014 that they were losing business to American farmers after Japan unexpectedly bypassed its usual Canadian suppliers and bought nearly forty-seven thousand tonnes of "U.S. hard wheat" allegedly because Canadian railways had failed, for the second month, to meet its contracted delivery deadlines.[13] The railway officials blamed the unusually cold weather of 2013–2014 for the delays.[14]

Their argument received an angry public response from the premier of Saskatchewan, Brad Wall. He stated that he had ordered a delegation of provincial ministers to meet with grain and railway companies to solve this urgent matter and complained: "This grain movement backlog is a very serious situation for the entire province and it is a high priority for our government. The delays in moving grain have led to lower prices for our producers at the farm gate and are harming our reputation as a reliable supplier of agriculture products thought out the world."[15]

Railways officials responded by again blaming the weather. They were sharply rebuffed by Premier Wall, who noted that cold winter weather had not blocked the flow of grains to ports in past years. He was supported by others who pointed to the lack of railway train engines and crews as the base problem, caused, according to an official of the Grain Millers Inc., by "… a much greater deal of the system being used by oil traffic" and thus the resulting reallocation of capacity from wheat to oil transportation.[16] As the complaints continued to mount, the federal government made an unprecedented decision in March 2014 and ordered the railways to immediately begin moving one million tonnes of grain per week under a threat of fines of up to $100,000 per day if they failed to comply with the order.[17]

The reality of the situation and who was to blame for the grain shipment difficulty will be settled eventually. The lesson to take away from the railways workers' strike threats and the 2013–2014 western grain experiences is the enormous importance the railways systems play in Canada's economy, a fact demonstrated by the urgency and authority with which the federal government moved to deal with these interruptions to railway transportation.

Imagine then an uncomplicated First Nations campaign of harassment: false alarms and interminable random calls to the police announcing that a section of a track had been dismantled somewhere in a lonely part of a line. Railways supervisors for safety reasons would have to immediately issue a "stop traffic order" to trains along the entire line until it had been inspected by railway crew — of course, escorted by armed security personnel — and declared safe.

Imagine the chaos in Canada if one or both national railways were blockaded not for five days in one area, as in British Columbia in 2012, but for weeks; or worse, "interrupted" sporadically nation-wide for months. Could the system handle a dozen such alerts every month? Do any informed members of the railways or the federal security bureaucracy doubt that such a situation would constitute a civil emergency requiring the continued deployment of the CF on "aid to the civil authority" missions? Think about it. Who has the initiative in our present situation?

Perhaps it would be appropriate for the federal government in the approaching circumstances to acknowledge the implicit legal and physical powers of the First Nations and deal with these facts before and not after a true national emergency "surprises" everyone. However, most Canadian politicians, military officers, police chiefs, and bureaucrats within the federal Integrated Terrorist Assessment Centre and Public Safety Canada[18] dismiss this vulnerability paradigm as imagined fantasy — in public anyway. Few media pundits give credence to the possibility either. Canadians, as is their right, however, should expect that federal and provincial ministers and their officials understand at least this reality: the First Nations formal and informal leaders do not see the notion of disrupting Canada's economy as a farfetched or impossible challenge, and their continual, if so far random, actions should be understood as warnings that "the fantasy" is alive among us.[19]

ANGRY VOICES HERALD
AN UNCERTAIN FUTURE

The hundreds of media reports and popular commentary concerning First Nations confrontations with Canadian politicians, federal authorities, and police seem like little more than a disjointed collection of unrelated incidents: a roadblock here, a stand-off there, angry statements by leaders and scolding responses from politicians — "sound and fury signifying nothing." Yet, there is a pattern in these events, a pattern that is in 2014 heading in one way: toward more demonstrations and confrontations and a gathering confidence in the First Nations communities that their causes can be advanced through the power of "activist politics."

The early confrontations in Oka, Gustafsen Lake, Ipperwash, Caledonia, and New Brunswick, and small-scale interferences with Canada's transportation systems elsewhere have created an activist vanguard of chiefs and intellectuals, and the (mostly) spontaneous Idle No More movement. The government's inability to construct a coherent strategy to deal with First Nations challenges and the reluctance of security forces at times to enforce the rule of law have demonstrated to Native activists that they and not governments command the limits of civil protest.

These challenges and the seeming impotence of governments to answer decisively only encourage more and perhaps more violent disruptions. In the spring of 2014, a squabble over the government's First Nations Control of First Nations Education Act led immediately to challenges not just to the details of the act itself, but to Canada's sovereignty. Derek Nepinak, Grand Chief of the Assembly of Manitoba Chiefs, denounced the government's proposed reform as "assimilationist and developed "… in the spirit of Canadian colonial lawmaking," in which every aspect of First Nations life is controlled by the minister of Aboriginal Affairs. "[I]ndigenous peoples living in Canada," he declared "have rights of self-determination recognized under international law ... [rights that this bill] blatantly denied."[20] The government, apparently shocked by this response, capitulated and withdrew the act. The overtly hostile reaction of First Nations leaders to the bill forced the resignation of AFN national chief Shawn Atleo, the resurrection of the dormant Confederacy of Nations — an alliance of First Nations subordinate to the AFN — and disorganization within the First Nations themselves.

The anger in the community was palpable. Declared one group of leaders: "Should Canada not withdraw and cease all imposed legislation on First Nations without our free, and prior and informed consent we will strategically and calculatedly begin the economic shutdown of Canada's economy from coast to coast."[21] The minister of AANDC unhelpfully responded in kind and asked the members of the House of Commons to "... condemn in the strongest terms the threat of those rogue chiefs who are threatening the security of Canada."[22]

The chiefs of the various First Nations could not agree on what approach they should take in this matter. Some urged caution and peacefulness while others were militant. The message to Canadians, however, was that the First Nations have discovered, as have other warriors through the ages, that the powers that have fallen into their hands come not from any great attributes they possess, but, ironically, from the weaknesses and disorganization of their much stronger opponent.

Canada's policies toward the First Nations have produced for citizens the very situation few could have conceived of in 1990 as the defeated Natives at Oka drifted back to their reserve. These policies, moreover, created from a downtrodden, dependant people the strong, united, and unforgiving society now standing fully armed on Canada's doorstep.

Pamela Palmater, an academic and one of the leading candidates to replace Chief Atleo as head of the AFN, described Canadian security officials (and, indirectly one supposes, certain non-Aboriginal academics) who suggest that it is the First Nations who are a potential threat to Canada as an outrageous irony:

> It was Canada and its Indian agents that were hostile and subversive to our peoples — not the other way around. It is we [the First Nations] who have premature deaths, worse health, less education, less employment and less access to land and resources. It is we who continue to suffer the intergenerational effects of their colonial laws and policies which STILL exist today.
>
> Can you get any more hostile that the over-apprehension of our children from our communities at three times the rate of residential schools? Or that some of federal prisons are populated 100 percent by Indigenous inmates or that the Indian Act still provides for our legislative extinction dates?
>
> Yet, we are supposed to be appeased when representatives of Canada speak about moving forward, looking ahead, and reconciliation. How can First Nations be expected to come to the table with any hope of making real progress when their treaty "partner"

comes to the table alleging good faith but
with no less than four federal departments
spying on our people and treating us like we
are terrorists on our own lands?[23]

Angry words can ignite spontaneous uprising. These types of
conflicts, however, most often simply burn themselves out
because they lack a focused object and coherent leadership.
For the moment, Canadians see in recent First Nations protests, such as, for instance, the 2013 Elsipogtog First Nation
shale gas riot in New Brunswick, disorganized, localized —
though violent — outbursts of anger that arise and then fade
away without much consequence for anyone, except, of course,
the arrested and jailed Natives. However, those who see these
skirmishes as examples of the limit of what we can expect to
endure in the future are watching the wrong channel.

The simmering discontent out on the land warns of a different kind of First Nations action in the future. Canadians
should be prepared to see and governments should be prepared
to counter blockades of Canada's major national transportation systems, the continued arming of major reserves, large
public demonstrations in major cities, confrontations between
First Nations "warriors" and police, leading in some cases to
provincial calls for "Aid of the Civil Powers" by the Canadian
Armed Forces, and other prolonged disruptions to national
peace, order, and public safety.

Some will scoff at suggestions that the First Nations community is capable of any significant actions that would harm
Canada. They might say: "The Natives simply don't have the

leadership to mount any such attack or the means to cause much harm." Such quick assessments ignore a critical factor. The First Nations community may well be weak in some important ways, but Canada's vulnerabilities more than compensate for this supposed weakness. The national transportation system — rail and road — running through sparely populated terrain is impossible to defend. Moreover, as we well know, much of the territory through which the Trans-Canada Highway and Canada's railways run, especially Northern Ontario and the northern regions of the Prairie provinces, is home to thousands of Native people. A small cohort of minimally trained "warriors" could close these systems in a matter of hours. Canada's cities, towns, and industries are dependant on the continuous transmission of electric power, often over long distances. These systems, too, are impossible to defend from sporadic interference. The so-called "security guarantee" provided by Canada's police and armed forces is simply too small to face down a widespread, clandestine rebel force.

The First Nations have sufficient means to wage a widespread, damaging insurgency against Canada, and Canada is especially vulnerable to such an uprising. Canadians' dismissive attitude towards Aboriginal people and ignorance of these facts of national life might not provoke a confrontation, but such an attitude might prevent governments from acting to forestall one and greatly increase the damage and the dangers if even a small-scale, but sustained, confrontation were to develop across most of Canada.

7

GETTING THINGS WRONG

"We have two choices: we can do things the hard way.
Or the harder way. There is no easy path."
— *AFN Chief Shawn A-in-chut Atleo*[1]

THE TRAJECTORY OF WARS
AMONG THE PEOPLE

Learning from experience in a potential or active insurgency environment can be very costly for everyone and pointlessly self-defeating as well. The history of insurgencies and so-called counter-insurgency operations (COIN) suggest that if the First Nations were to attempt to advance their sovereignty ambitions by unlawful means — for instance, by mounting a prolonged campaign to disable Canada's national transportation systems — they would inevitably be confronted by an aggressive, armed response from the federal government. The same history suggests also that if the federal government were to act pre-emptively and aggressively to counter a suspected or nascent First Nations insurgency, Canada would inevitably face a unified, armed, and economically devastating response from the First Nations, the very outcome a pre-emptive policy was meant to forestall.

No one will benefit if the latent anger and confusion in our communities propels our peoples into a serious national confrontation. Ask yourself: Why would an advanced society allow itself to be herded sheep-like down a road to hostilities when the inevitable end of such hostilities — as Canadian and First Nations leaders already understand — would be a political settlement of some sort? Why would leaders not begin to create the framework of such a political settlement today, before a catastrophic, irrational insurgency overwhelms common sense tomorrow?

Most essays exploring insurgencies begin, as we have already described, on the assumption that "greed and grievances" are the root causes of our unhappiness; or on the assumption, as Professor Paul Collier and his Oxford colleagues argue, that insurgencies erupt when a combination of determinants make them feasible. These concepts, highlighting motive and opportunity, are helpful to our understanding of why insurgencies happen. However, we can't separate these ideas from others that aid our understanding of why insurgencies fail and why they end. Constructing an effective national strategy aimed at deterring or defeating an insurgency requires an integrated analysis drawn from all these perspectives.

Consider the trajectories of the significant insurgencies of the twentieth century and more recent operations, as in Afghanistan. The *successful* anti-colonial upheavals of this era, for example, in Indonesia, Algeria, Cyprus, Kenya, and in Vietnam, especially during the anti-French campaign in the 1950s, followed a generally predictable path: armed colonial/ dictatorial policing and suppression; internal, anti-government political agitation; police (backed at times by military units) raids on insurgent areas and the arrest of rebel leaders; increased public violence; small and large, insurgent counterattacks on the government establishment, the police, and the economy; raising popular anti-establishment support; ever bigger, but ultimately ineffective, military counterinsurgency operations; the deterioration of the government's control over large areas; the collapse of domestic and international support; and then, in the cited examples, outright victory for the rebellious side. Stalemates are uncommon in these types of insurgencies, though at some point during long campaigns, one side or the other may put an offer to negotiate on the table.

General Smith's "wars among the people," as in Spain in the 1930s, Ireland over many decades, the Balkans in the 1990s, South Africa over a long period ending in 1990, and the conflict in Afghanistan, follow a different trajectory than anti-colonial insurgencies because of their different characteristics. Generally, these civil wars evolve from uncompromising combat first to stalemate and then, perhaps, to negotiations from which a new political regime arises. The reality of the "fight first and negotiate later" strategy in wars amongst the people is that in most cases, the final, politically acceptable outcome was more or less foreseeable before the fighting began. The tragedy is that these predictable outcomes had to be "discovered" in negotiations after the waste of a great deal of blood and treasure.

Twin fatal assumptions reside simultaneously for both sides in the "fight first" strategy. The initial hypothesis is that defeating one's opponent in battle can settle affairs without the give and take risks inherent in negotiations. The corollary argues that even if one side cannot defeat its opponent entirely, it can bring down sufficient death and destruction on the opponent's forces and the economy that he will be forced to ask for negotiations, and thus it will be able to negotiate from a position of superior strength against his opponent's obvious weakness.

Such logic almost immediately transforms a civil/political dispute into a quasi-military or completely military endeavour that tends to compromise and sideline the underlying political aims of both or all parties. Warfare, especially when opponents are more or less evenly capable, thus becomes the dominant aim of the insurgency itself. Perhaps societies have learned, if they have learned anything, that "negotiate first, fight as a last resort," is always the better premise on which to build a pre-emptive counter-insurgency strategy.

When constructing strategies to confront an insurgency, the underlying idea to hold close is that insurgencies in their many manifestations are always aimed at transforming the status quo. Counter-insurgency operations are unlikely to succeed if their only purpose is to counter transformation. A successful COIN strategy would be based on ideas — mostly sociopolitical ideas, not military ones — aimed not at incrementally "mending holes in … obsolete legislative frameworks," but at implementing fundamentally transformative ideas that produce public policy outcomes meant to undercut popular support for those who would impose change at the point of a gun.[2] Nothing is as disheartening for a radical rebel as a political opponent who sees merit in the rebel's point of view and agrees to discuss it peacefully.

BEGINNING FROM THE END

Preparing to avoid the possibility of an insurgency typically begins, for those in the "greed and grievance" school, with an assessment of underlying complaints; for those of the "feasibility determinants" persuasion, preparation begins with an examination of the determining factors. In the first case, strategists might decide to redress grievances; in the second, a plan to reduce or even eliminate the feasibilities that might enable an uprising might be considered. A play-it-safe planner might tackle both premises as parts of a comprehensive approach. Such assessments would, of course, require a concurrent analysis of the opponent's several capabilities, strengths, and weaknesses. With this information in hand, the government would have the framework for negotiations or a counter-insurgency strategy.

This seemingly logical front-end methodology, however, would be incomplete if it did not include at least a detailed description of a participant's desired endgame. In other words, in the context of a Canadian-First Nations conflict, leaders on both sides would want to answer this tricky question: What is it politically and economically that we, Canada, or we, the First Nations, hold dear and, consequentially, that we would not offer up for negotiation or surrender? Commanders would like to know, as well, at what point their political leaders would declare victory, given that in an insurgency the contest is not likely to end with one side or the other raising a white flag in surrender. Insurgency leaders must know when they would be willing to begin negotiating or cease fighting. Likewise, every political leader and strategist must also consider the seemingly unthinkable before an insurgency begins; that is, at what point would he agree to negotiate with the insurgents or, in the worst of all cases, concede defeat.

"No military operation ever unfolds as planned" is a much-ignored military maxim. Insurgencies with significant consequences at stake have been lost because political and military planners placed too much faith in their initial plans even as circumstances changed, sometimes radically and suddenly. Careful strategic planners — usually collaborating in some form of political, military, and police joint staff — must attempt to appreciate how an operation or a campaign might develop over time and then build into their plans sufficient flexibility to allow commanders to adjust to unexpected enemy moves or to exploit unexpected opportunities. Building such flexibility into the end-game of a counter-insurgency strategy or campaign, however, is particularly difficult because assessing and planning based estimations about how an insurgency might end — assuming it will not end in the outright defeat of the insurgent's military force — is a complicated, not-well-understood phenomenon.

GETTING THINGS WRONG: THE FEDERAL GOVERNMENT

"Getting it wrong" — aimless political dithering by leaders in one or both communities — will surely expose, as it already has, the nation and the First Nations to many more years of turmoil, perhaps even violent turmoil. Policy errors or arbitrary decisions that appear to favour some over others will encourage radicals and, as the history of insurgencies confirms in blood, radicals on one side beget radicals on the other side — to everyone's misfortune.

In most discussions about errant public policy, the concentrated efforts of bureaucrats, commissions of inquiry, and so on, are usually directed towards the examination of the mechanics of the policy, that is, to its administrative costs, delivery, and relevance to wider political interests. As reasonable as this bureaucratic routine might seem in the moment, serious policy problems occur not simply because of the particulars of the policy — its ways and means and rules and procedures — but because there are flaws that reside rather in the conceptual framework underpinning the policy and in the organizational structure designed to manage policy. In other words, policy outcomes rarely, if ever, reflect precisely the intent of their founding idea or ideas.

Policy is the product of ideas, managed by actors with authority to decide, working within an organizational hierarchy according to established procedures and rules. Changing outcomes in complex public policy fields requires amendment or, at times, radical changes in the concept framework underlying the policy and/or a comprehensive restructuring of the actor/organization/process. No one should expect a government white paper on Indian Affairs announcing fundamentally new policy aspirations based on radical or even simply new ideas to deliver any such thing if the implementation of the policy is placed in the hands of a bureaucracy that is structurally unfit or a bureaucrat who is intellectually incapable of managing transformational change.

The following is a brief summary of key, but troubled, government First Nations policies that show how the government has failed to effect necessary change in a number of important areas. This summary is not meant to suggest policy solutions (some such ideas will be offered in the next chapter). Rather, the purpose here is to expose major policy areas that are in desperate need of reform. What is needed is a change in approach to reform, away from the simple "Is this good policy?" point of view that focuses on addressing individual issues, to a starkly holistic, concept-structure-outcome approach.

SOVEREIGNTY

It is likely safe to assume that any future federal government will continue the policy of the government in 2014 and anchor its strategies and polices regarding Canada-First Nations relations in the principle that Canada is a sovereign state and that the First Nations, singularly or collectively, are not sovereign as the term is understood in international relations. Even though the government recognizes, in law and regulations, the idea that the First Nations have an "inherent right of self-government," it is the federal government, ultimately, that defines in fact and effect the federal structure — the Indian Act, AANDC, and the powers of the minister to establish rules and regulations — that set the boundaries around the concept of inherent rights.

Thus, Canada will continue to insist that the government, acting within the Canadian Constitution and the law, alone has final jurisdiction over national policies with regard to the First Nations and in any dispute beyond what is recognized by regulations as an "inherent right" of the First Nations. Should any First Nations chose to define itself as a "distinct society," it would, nevertheless, remain subordinate to that idea and intent.

Continuing, however, to base Canada's relationships with the First Nations on the idea that the people are in every respect simply a conquered group of Canadians is inevitably dangerous. The idea defines "getting it wrong" in Canadian-First Nations relations. Any policy based in such a concept would immediately provide agitators with an issue they could use to rally the people to reject even the idea of inherent right of self-government — "a legal trick" according to one influential Native activist. Such an attempt would be regarded across most of the Aboriginal communities in Canada as an unjust and arbitrary limitation to their right of sovereignty and, thus, to every other aspect of their social and political lives. The central issue facing Canada and First Nations is discovering how to integrate meaningfully competing concepts — sovereignty and the inherent right of self-government — without unravelling Canada's hard-won, complex constitution.

THE INDIAN ACT

Few Canadians and not many First Nations people have much more than a passing awareness of the Indian Act, that "Victorian horror," the largely discredited but still all-embracing act of Parliament that defines who is an "Indian" and controls absolutely, even 150 years after it was first established, most aspects of First Nations life in Canada.[3] As noted in earlier chapters, the act subordinates the people to the office of the federal minister of Aboriginal and Northern Affairs Canada. Even though some leaders in the First Nations community support reluctantly the existence of some articles of the act, it is built on a framework of ideas meant to control First Nations people and most every aspect of their everyday lives, and to subjugate the Native people to the Canadian state.

The Indian Act, when conceived, was to "Indians" in Canada the same in many ways as slave legislation and laws were to "Negros" in the United States before the emancipation (at least in law) of African Americans more than one hundred years ago.[4] But, of course, that legislation and those laws no longer inform public policy in America, unlike the Indian Act in Canada.

Honest attempts to amend or repeal entirely the act have been stymied, not just by governments of all stripes but, ironically, also by the insistence of many influential Native leaders that it must stay on the books until it is replaced by legislation that protects First Nations rights implicitly recognized within the act. Others, usually non-Aboriginal Canadians, suggest that the Indian Act inhibits the people from enjoying the rights and liberties Canadians enjoy, and, therefore, should be abolished. For instance, well-intentioned people suggest that the act be discarded so that people resident on reserves would be able to own their own homes on these lands much as Canadians can own homes and property most anywhere in Canada.[5]

This suggested administrative fix to the act, and others like it, are resisted by First Nations leaders because such ideas are incompatible with the concept of a communal society: the fundamental and traditional organizing principle of First Nations life before the arrival of white settlers, and, still today, a safeguard for many traditions. The danger in this idea, as First Nations people see it and others like it, is assimilation — adoption of Western models, such as those for land ownership, will draw First Nations people away from their concept of traditional life and move them into the overpowering concepts and practices of Canada's multicultural society.

Canada's relations and negotiations with the First Nations are hamstrung by the Indian Act, however. It restricts the freedoms and sovereignty of the First Nations and serves as a continuing wound to the pride and esteem of the people. On the other hand, it binds the hands of well-meaning federal legislators. At its worst, the act holds people captive in disabling social circumstances at the very time opportunities for independent economic and social advancement are arriving in distant First Nations reserves.

For instance, government policy required, until 2006, that the leaders of a First Nations community seek the approval of the minister of AANDC to spend any money earned from its land and natural resources. Under the 2006 First Nations Oil and Gas and Money Management Act, the government now *allows* each community "to manage its own finances, including royalties from oil, mining, and gas [earnings]."[6] This not-so-new policy is a good step in the right direction, but it still carries the stigma of paternalism because a First Nation must present to the minister a financial plan before the minister will give a community access to the dispensation provided for in the Oil and Gas Act. Moreover, its implementation has been so slow that its effect on the First Nations as a whole has been and likely will continue to be barely visible for years to come — witness the 2014 celebration of the implementation of the first such agreement under that act eight years after it was enacted![7]

The Indian Act (see Chapter Three) is a trap waiting to ensnare governments and the First Nations in a self-defeating conflict, yet the federal government and some First Nations leaders seem content to allow this danger to direct their collective futures.

TREATIES AND LAND TITLE

Few issues involving First Nations and Canada attract more acrimony and hostility than quarrels over land and who has title to it. Today's difficulties — legal, political, and social — are the consequences of the imperfect transfer of jurisdiction over land title following the British assumption of sovereignty in North America in 1763. It is also part of a long story of settlers' and their governments' exploitation of First Nations and their land. If Canadians and the First Nations are to live together peacefully they must, together, even after all these years, reach forward and correct this imperfection in our society.

The history and the content of Canada's treaties with the First Nations are, to say the least, complex. Among other complicating considerations, negotiators today wishing to revise existing treaties or create new ones must acknowledge and work within the shadow of a history dating to 1763 and the straightjacket placed on them by existing treaties and laws, especially the Royal Proclamation of 1763 and Section 35 of the Constitution Act of 1982. Both sides must also be mindful of the near certainty that new agreements, once concluded, will be binding on Canadians and the First Nations people far into the unknowable future. The negotiations are not simple, nation-to-nation bilateral matters, but involve concurrent dealings with scores of First Nations and a host of policy questions that both sides must assume will have significant constitutional, legal, economic, social, and cultural consequences for Canada and the First Nations — and, in some case, for Inuit and Métis communities as well — for generations to come.

Between 1871 and 1921, the Crown entered into treaties with various First Nations to open Western and Northern Canada to settlement and agriculture and resource development. These treaties (numbered 1–11) moved the Native people off the land and into reserves and promised to provide them with, among other things, animals, farming instruments, grants of money, and rights to hunt and fish. The First Nations who signed these treaties and others who hold signed treaties are referred to as "Treaty First Nations." Canada's position is that these treaties are settled and not generally open to new negotiations.[8]

Today, treaty policy and negotiations in Canada are centred on "modern treaties," comprehensive land claim settlements, and specific claims. Comprehensive land claim settlements deal with areas of Canada where Aboriginal people's claims have not been addressed by treaty, or other legal means. By 2013, a full forty years after the land claims regime was announced, the federal government had settled twenty-six comprehensive claims with Aboriginal people "covering roughly 40 percent of Canada's land mass. Assessments and negotiations of dozens of other claims are ongoing in 2014.

Specific claims "… arise when there is an outstanding historical grievance between a First Nation and the Crown that relates to an unfulfilled obligation of a treaty or another agreement, or a breach of statutory responsibilities by the Crown."[9] Governments have recently made impressive progress towards settling these outstanding claims. In 2007, 50 percent of these types of claims were "under assessment" (meaning, as noted in one government paper, "… not going anywhere") and a mere 10 percent of active claims had been "concluded." As of March 2013, however, only 7 percent of specific claims were still under assessment, while 16 percent were in negotiations, and 77 percent had been settled.[10]

If the government has had success in negotiating treaties and land claims, it has had considerably less success in living up to the commitments it has made in those treaties. "Canada," the federal government declares, "is committed to honouring its lawful obligations to First Nations."[11] Yet, there is not much honour in a commitment, for instance, to promise under treaties completed in the late nineteenth and early twentieth centuries to provide land to First Nations and then not surrender all of the lands agreed upon to the First Nations until forced to do so almost one hundred years later.

Complaints based on several "oversights" on the part of the federal and Manitoba governments, for instance, involving thousands of acres of valuable land (most now in the hands of the Crown, municipalities, and Canadian citizens), are finally being given redress under the 1997 Canada-Manitoba Treaty Land Entitlement Agreement (TLE). This agreement has so far resulted in settlements with the twenty-nine affected Manitoba First Nations with the resulting transfer of up to 1.4 million acres in additional land to the associated reserves and the payment of more than $190 million. As of April 1, 2013, sixteen years after the signing of the TLE, an estimated 4.5 million acres of entitlement land has been identified and/or "set aside" for the First Nations, but several agreements have yet to be finalized.

In 2013, however, the federal government suddenly decided to, in effect, withdraw from the entire process due to complications caused by its "duty to consult" responsibilities.[12] In business and treaty making, "getting it wrong" is defined as "not getting it done."

SELF-GOVERNMENT

The First Nations' "inherent right to self-government" is another complicated and complicating matter in Canada-First Nations relations. The Government of Canada has recognized the inherent right of self-government as an existing Aboriginal right under Section 35 of the Constitution Act, 1982.[13] As a constitutional right, Aboriginal self-government is, of course, protected by the courts. However, although the Government of Canada "acknowledges that the inherent right of self-government may be enforceable through the courts," its preferred approach is to address this pivotal issue through negotiations. Nevertheless, Canada set boundaries around this right, intentionally constraining the breadth and extent of this recognition: "... [the] Aboriginal peoples of Canada have a right to government themselves in relations to matters that are internal to their communities and integral to their unique cultures, identities, traditions, languages and institutions and with respect to their special relationships to their land and their resources.[14]

Furthermore, Canada has placed a number of sovereign safeguards on the exercise of Aboriginal inherent rights by declaring that these rights must be exercised "... within the framework of the Canadian Constitution." The federal government has acted also to protect provincial governments and territorial governments by making them "... necessary parties to negotiations and agreements where subject matters being negotiated normally fall within provincial [or territorial] jurisdiction," and, third, it has emphasized the commanding sovereignty of Canada by its specific direction that "... the inherent right of self-government does not include a right of sovereignty in the international law sense, and will not result in sovereign independent Aboriginal nation states."[15]

The government of Canada faces continual and continuing challenges to its Aboriginal policies and its approaches to Aboriginal rights and governance. It has acted over the years to accommodate change and the decisions of the courts while at the same time vigorously defending Canada's constitutional rights and at the so-called "public interest." All of this has been seen, however, as too little by Canada's Native community. Government accommodation and its protection of Canada's sovereign rights and the public's interests has often led to disputes with the First Nations, who believe themselves sovereign and, thus, the rightful guarantors of their peoples' interests.

There are, of course, several avenues open to governments to help them formulate public policy, but, in some cases, governments may feel compelled to act arbitrarily. Doing so, however, may inflame a dispute rather than resolve it — the failed First Nations education act of 2014 is an example. Getting it wrong, in a policy-making sense — and this applies not only to Aboriginal affairs — is exemplified, for example, by governments' failures to consult involved parties or to reveal information to citizens, and, especially, by unreasonable decisions to use the power of Parliament or of the majority to impose an unpopular policy on less-powerful or vulnerable Canadians.

NATIONAL SECURITY

How a public policy issue is characterized by government leaders often prescribes how it will be treated. That aphorism is exemplified by the manner in which federal governments over the years have dealt with disputes between Canadians and the First Nations.

There have certainly been enough "situations" since 1970 to suggest to some people that the federal government is facing a significantly more threatening Canada-First Nations national security problem than existed formerly. Civil demonstrations, road and railway blockades, challenges to Canadian laws and authority over cigarette sales, for instance, as well as other such activities by First Nations people might tempt the Canadian law and order establishment to suggest to the government that it is, indeed, on the cusp of a national security threat. If that notion were to take hold and form a major part of any national Aboriginal strategy, then the thought might truly become the father of a dangerous policy.[16]

It should be stated that thinking about the disagreements between some First Nations leaders and Canadian politicians in terms of national security is not, in the circumstances, entirely unreasonable. Announcing a national First Nations policy centred on the idea that Canada in 2014 is confronted by a unified, armed insurrection and taking aggressive counter-actions against it would, however, be unwise. Yet, there are hints that the government, or perhaps some free-ranging government agents, is working in that direction. Leaders of the Idle No More movement report that "[T]here has been an increase in the use of non-traditional tactics by CSIS [Canadian Security and Intelligence Service] to get one-on-one time from various indigenous activists."[17]

If this is true, then it is worrying. CSIS is prohibited by law from spying on citizens unless they have clear reasons for doing so. Such activities must be authorized by senior CSIS officials before any actions are taken.[18] Assuming that the agents in question were acting officially, then one could only conclude that groups of Native people waving flags as they walk down public streets in Canada are considered by CSIS and, therefore, the government as a national security risk. Getting it wrong occurs when politicians or officials mistake or exaggerate peaceful protests as harbingers of a national security threats, and, thus, risk, among other things, enflaming an already uneasy relationship between First Nations people and agitated, suspicious Canadians.

PUBLIC AND SOCIAL SERVICES

The social security situation in most First Nations communities is, or should be, a national scandal; unfortunately, for the most part it is not something that stirs most Canadians to any kind of action. It is, however, a menacing national security scandal, because claims of unfair treatment — legitimate or otherwise — made by First Nations leaders tends to excite hostile reactions from Canadians who hold a contrary view. The details of "life on the res" were explained in earlier chapters as were the links between this situation and the grievance and feasibility theories of insurgencies. This sorry history and its effects on First Nations people, and especially vulnerable young people, is not a story about a poor nation struggling to find resources enough to properly feed, clothe, educate, and care for its citizens. It's the story of a rich nation's neglect of its citizens.

Moreover, it's a story of condemning public reports that time and again record the dreadful conditions of the people — mostly, but not exclusively, on-reserve — and of numerous governments' indifferent, responsibility-dodging responses. Getting things wrong in this context means excusing the situation as a matter of dollars and cents, or necessary government regulations, or the unavoidable outcome of complicated treaty rights and payouts, or, unforgivably, the fault of the victims. Getting this issue wrong is, at best, willful neglect, and, at worst, (to borrow a phrase) a clear and present danger to Canada's national security, because it provides the base for radical Natives to tear apart Canada's already problematic relationship with the First Nations.

CRIME AND PUNISHMENT

The incarceration of Aboriginal people in Canada's jails and prisons is, or ought to be, a stunning national disgrace. Besides the waste of human lives that is the necessary result of incarceration for many individuals, these inmates while in custody and on release play a significant role in the development and perpetuation of criminal gangs across Canada. There have been no useful attempts by government during the last several decades to address either the factors that contribute to these high incarceration rates or to develop a national policy that might redress the wide negative social and security implications of Canada's obviously failed "justice system." The failures of governments to even attempt to develop a comprehensive policy to reform this Aboriginal crime and criminal-producing factory, or to provide, in the meantime, practical and effective alternatives to the long-term jailing of Aboriginal people is a glaring example of a federal system content to maintain policies aimed at getting things wrong.

GETTING THINGS WRONG: THE FIRST NATIONS

The purpose of the following consideration of policy wrongheadedness on the part of some key First Nations leaders is presented not to be "fair" or to achieve a necessary balancing of federal and First Nations governance rights and wrongs. Rather, it is an acknowledgement of the reality that getting things wrong is not the private preserve of the federal government and that getting things right (or at least making things somewhat better) will inevitably require co-operation between the two parties.

Far from being helpless wards of the state, First Nations, individually and collectively, enjoy considerable discretion over how they organize their political and social lives and how they manage their communities' affairs. The election or appointment of chiefs, for example, varies from nation to nation. Some have "customary" or "hereditary" chiefs, who are more or less appointed for life, while other bands may elect their chiefs (men or women) under their own rules and procedures. Customary traditions and concepts derived from Native knowledge influence many or most of a community's affairs as well.

Aboriginal people are no longer absolute captives of the Indian Act or beholden to an "Indian Agent." The federal government still retains considerable discretionary powers to intervene in First Nations' affairs. The minister of AANDC, for example, can on the minister's initiative assume "third party management" of any reserve the minister believes to be dysfunctional, or replace a chief suspected of misdirecting funds or other malpractices. Nevertheless, considerable policy discretion has been passed, formally and informally, from the federal government to the people, allowing First Nations to make decisions within their own communities. Natives are, increasingly, excising their rights of self-government, not only at the band level but also quasi-nationally, engaging on a broad range of issues when, for instance, they elect national or regional chiefs and when they insist on meeting collectively with the prime minister of Canada and other national leaders.

This more or less formal regime — decentralized rule by the Indian Act — is not now as all-commanding as some Native leaders and some outsiders have long complained of it as being. Today, a radically new intergovernmental regime constructed on a unique conceptual framework of "modern treaties" and the inherent right to self-government is rapidly evolving across Canada. In the best of future times, "getting it right" will no longer be the responsibility of the federal government — that duty will fall to the First Nations. It would be an enormous tragedy for the young adults and children of the First Nations community if the government were to finally grant their leaders the powers they have fought so long and hard for only to have that change lead to a no-change, dead-end society.

The rehabilitation of the First Nations community, one would hope, will begin with a frank acknowledgement by the elders of the failures of the leaders in so many of their communities. It was not the Indian Act, for instance, that allowed drug dealers and criminals access to young people on-reserve. Bureaucrats in Ottawa are not responsible when reserve leaders stand aside as alcohol abuse runs almost unchecked in Native communities. The failure of leaders to actually lead their communities is a not inconsequential reason for why First Nations fail. Getting things right for the First Nations requires leaders who lead honestly, forcefully, and by example.

COMMUNITY ACTION PLANS

In a crisis, or, preferably, before a crisis demolishes a reserve, community leaders should establish plans to remove individuals who trade in illicit drugs, medicines, and alcohol; persuade children to remain in school to the end of high school; organize community self-help, home safety, and renovation projects; establish community elder/chronically ill safety programs; and build accountable, elected community leadership initiatives.

SELF-GOVERNMENT ACTION PLANS

The concept of self-government cannot be implemented in the absence of administrative competence, capability, and capacity. The First Nations cannot succeed or even remain healthy as a collection of small, scattered, economically non-viable, reserve-based communities. In the early twenty-first century, and as part of the modern economic/commercial society that is Canada, small reserves, and especially isolated "fly-in" reserves, will be dependent societies forever. The services people need — doctors and hospitals and routine access to other health care facilities; police and fire services; schools and teachers covering education from entry to the end of high school (at least); public administrators; and so on — cannot be adequately (to say nothing about economically) provided to remote communities. A First Nations directed plan to consolidate remote First Nations is an essential requirement if the First Nations are to prosper from the benefits offered by self-government. Getting it right in this case means the relocation of scores of non-viable reserves.

Many people, with varying interests at stake, might argue that the predicted natural resources boom expected to develop across remote areas of Canada in the next twenty years will turn small, remote First Nations into viable communities. Perhaps it will. In the meantime, however, how will the First Nations community assure the welfare of the inhabitants of these totally dependent reserves until the good times roll?

A FIRST NATIONS POLITICAL STRUCTURE

The First Nations are entering a new era, with increased powers and, rather unusual for the community, specific responsibilities.

Again, the modern treaties, specific claims, and TLE agreements are resulting in an increase in the wealth of many First Nations communities. The expansion of many reserves — in some case by millions of acres, the development of urban reserves, the increasing importance of comprehensive self-government arrangements, and the complexities of "responsibility to consult" provisions will together place enormous stresses on the present, rather disjointed First Nations political structure.

The current First Nations political structure is composed of 617 independent and equal "nations," some with thousands of members but many with only a few hundred souls. These nations are united only by the fact that they were the original inhabitants in Canada. In the international legal sense, there never was and there is not today a united "Indian" nation in Canada. The quirks of history, for both the First Nations and for Canada, led to the awkward establishment of one internationally recognized state, Canada, that includes 617 self-proclaimed First Nations and, of course, Inuit communities and Métis nations too. Canadians have proved that they can live with this arrangement for better or worse. But can the First Nations?

In the evolving circumstances resulting from modern treaties, decisions by the Supreme Court of Canada, and the federal government's policy innovations, First Nations face considerable challenges and ever-present possibilities to get things wrong. In an assembly of 617 nations with greatly different histories, treaty rights, and developing economic power, who speaks for the greater good? Real power is rarely wielded by coalitions of the small and weak mixed in with the large and powerful. Divisions among coalition leaders provide to an external challenger a vulnerability to be exploited. For instance, the government could attempt to weaken a First Nations coalition by offering attractive benefits to some and none to the others.

The National Assembly of First Nations (AFN) is such a coalition. It is weakened by its composition and its consensual-style leadership by the lack of a unifying leader. Indeed, the AFN has no leader in the governmental sense; the national chief of the AFN is merely a coordinating spokesperson. The so-called "national chief" has no ability to impose a position on anyone and especially not on any coalition if there was a disagreement amongst the chiefs. The abrupt and, some suggest, forced resignation of Shawn Atleo as national chief of the AFN in the spring of 2014 sharply illustrates this point. The power of the AFN (such as it is) lies in the hands of the 617 band chiefs, who, by consensus decide the issues of the day. The disunity implicit in the consensus concept weakens the First Nations, a weakness prime ministers have used to their advantage when it serves their purposes.

Building strength for the political battles to come demands that the First Nations develop a modern political structure, a Confederacy of the First Nations, perhaps founded on the ideas of unity of purpose and unity of effort. There is no other way in which the power of the First Nations can be maximized and there is no other way the First Nations will be able to exploit the natural resources riches of their lands.

8

DISARMING THE TIME BOMB

"At the root of the issues is the persistent claim by
the [First Nations] that they are sovereign states. It is
hard to see anything ahead but capitulation [by one
side or the other] or bloodshed if the issue is forced."[1]

Research aimed at understanding why insurgencies begin and
how they end suggests four approaches that Canadian and
First Nations leaders (working together if possible) might consider to avert a First Nations insurgency that would surely be a
national disaster. These conceptual approaches include redressing
underlying grievances; acting to degrade or minimize the "determinants" that make an insurgency feasible; waiting passively
for time to diminish the threat; and developing with the First
Nations a "negotiate first" *pre-emptive strategy* aimed at reaching
agreements that will disarm the time bomb in our future.

If grievances are the triggers for the bomb, then eliminat-
ing these "root causes" will disarm the threat. This idea, as

noted earlier, is challenged as incoherent, especially since any attempts to alleviate grievances can be subject to hijacking by advocacy groups with their own pet agendas. Even the process of judging the merits of various grievances in order to determine which ones deserve attention first can become a complex undertaking, one that leads to even more grievances, concerning, for instance, the fairness of the adjudicating proceedings and/or the adequacy of the outcome.

Settlements meant to resolve particular complaints may encourage piggyback demands from other groups or communities unrelated to the initiating body. Grouped grievances, apparently solved, sometimes merely set the table for new grievances, arising from the dissatisfaction of one party or another with the agreed settlement. Broad-based grievances, especially where the links between issues and communities are not obvious, can muddy remedial procedures and encourage competitions between communities. The current difficulties between various First Nations and other bodies concerning an agreement regarding the construction of the so-called Northern Gateway project in British Columbia is an example of these types of commotion.[2]

At times, discussions concerning a particular grievance may become entangled in a web of individual complaints, special interests, and ethnic, legal, and procedural confusions. Grievances, moreover, are subject to what, in another field, is termed the "snowball effect" — a term that describes the tendency of some "… [policy] activities naturally … to grow to inordinate size and unless positive control is maintained this growth continues until, like a ball of wet snow, a huge accumulation of slush obscures the hard core of essential [matters]."[3] For example, the government's 2013–2014 attempts to frame a new

First Nations education policy became entangled in the much broader — and typically obscure — issues such as consultations, traditional rights, and the place of the national chief of the Assembly of First Nations in the assessment of the new policy.

As the feasibility theory notes, however, the mere existence of a grievance, or even a host of grievances, does not inevitably ignite an insurgency. On the other hand, in situations where a particular grievance is mistakenly defined as a potential cause for an insurgency, settling that particular grievance rather than the actual underlying cause will not prevent an insurgency from erupting. Although governments need to provide, as they do in most cases today, open, accessible, and fair mechanisms through which citizens can seeking redress for their complaints, using the bare bones of the greed and grievance theory as a basis for a counter-insurgency strategy to deal with the threat of insurgencies in Canada today is unlikely to stop the ticking of the time bomb's clock.

Given that the hypothesis, "[I]f an insurgency is feasible, then it will occur," has not been disproved, the determinants that contribute to an insurgency's feasibility must, in some way, be disabled. The critical assumption embedded in this theory is that a state, the common target of insurgencies, has the power and the means to make harmless these enabling determinants. Any assessment of the feasibility of an insurgency in a society that concludes that the state does not in fact have such powers may present political leaders with some rather uncertain choices.

Even where a government has the power and means to develop a pragmatic national strategy to combat a feasibility-based insurgency, getting the strategy right and maintaining its objectives over time while under the stress of competing ideas and demands is a complex undertaking. Political leaders and their advisors would need to consider a number of fundamental questions before (one would hope) they confront a real or apprehended insurgency.

For example: To what degree is the nation vulnerable to the underlying determinants as defined in the feasibility theory? What, therefore, is the strategic objective, the desired end-state, of the national counter-feasibility strategy? How might each vulnerable determinant be neutralized or otherwise made harmless? What economic, security, and legal means are available to address the objectives of the strategy? What social and economic boundaries and military rules of engagement should be placed on counter-feasibility operations? What propaganda programs will be necessary to maintain public support for these inevitably intrusive counter-insurgency operations; and what programs will need to be developed to win the hearts and minds of the insurgents' supporters in order to diminish their aid and assistance to the conflict?

Of the five determinants of feasibility, the federal government today, acting prudently in co-operation with willing First Nations, has the means and authority to take steps to significantly reduce three factors originating in the First Nations community, factors that, left untended, could lead to a First Nations challenge to Canada's sovereignty.[4] The government, as a matter of priority, could develop and fund programs aimed at decreasing the social, economic, and political fractionalization gap between Canadian and First Nations people. Second, Canada might promptly develop and deliver education and training programs to prepare and encourage the integration into the Canadian economy of significant numbers of the rapidly growing Native 15–24 YOA cohort. Such programs, if successfully implemented, would put these young people beyond the reach of radical, and possibly insurgent, leaders, and would, thus, diminish the "warrior cohort" threat building in many communities.

Greater attention could be paid also to increasing the safety and well-being of people on-reserve by immediately reinforcing the credibility of the "security guarantee" in First Nations communities. Such a program would require enhanced training and structural reorganization of on-reserve police services, and greater integration of these services with local and provincial police units. Governments and their officials talk about these types of programs, but the product of such talk generally have no substance, or are, in bureaucratic-speak, "still under development," or are befuddled by the myriad intricacies of hundreds of self-government agreements.

Two critical feasibility determinants — Canada's topography, making offence easy and defence very difficult; and Canada's economic dependence on natural resources and the necessity to transport them to markets over long distances on isolated, vulnerable transportation networks — are matters over which governments have very little influence. The country's topography, obviously, is not a candidate for reform, meaning it cannot be remade to create a land more easily defensible. Governments cannot reorder in any significant and economically practicable way the nation's transportation-dependent export and import trade.

In fact, the country's dependence on natural resources exports is likely to grow in the next decades and, directly or indirectly, make the Canadian economy proportionally even more vulnerable than it is today. The most obvious remedy to First Nations threats to interfere with these vital components of the Canadian economy is to integrate the Native people of Canada into this economy; that is, in a number of ways make them partners in the nation's primary businesses and offer them a share of the wealth that flows from them.

WAIT AND SEE WHAT HAPPENS

History suggests, generally, that insurrections end in one of four ways: in victory — the unconditional surrender of the ruling government and its supporter to the insurgents (Algeria, Vietnam, and Cuba); second, in the defeat of the insurgent leadership and its supporters (the Riel rebellion and Sri Lanka, 2009); three, with the parties negotiating and settling the dispute through some sort of a "final agreement" (South Africa, Ireland, India); or, finally, with the insurgency simply petering out and fading away or continuing sporadically for years to some sort of inconclusive ending, as seems to be the trajectory of the insurgencies in Syria and sub-Saharan Africa today.

Designing a national strategy to guide a COIN operation depends on the strategist's understanding and/or assessment of the present and future state of the insurgency the nation faces. Generally, if an insurgency is just beginning to establish itself in a community, then a deliberate attack on its capabilities — people, logistical support systems, and intelligence capabilities — might forestall the insurgency all together. If, on the other hand, an insurgency has already embedded itself in a supporting society, grown its popular base, and attracted and trained recruits — in other words, if it has consolidated its base of operations — then it will be much more difficult and costly for counter-insurgency commanders to degrade their opponent's capabilities and root them out of the supporting community. The strategic dilemma for political leaders and commanders in the early stages of an insurgency is that if they move too early and too aggressively they may drive the population into the hands of the insurgents. Moving too late, on the other hand, may allow the insurgents time to establish and consolidate their base, making a COIN campaign practically unwinnable.

An assessment of the present state of First Nations capabilities to resist the government's authority, especially in First Nations territory — exemplified by road and rail blockades and other economic interferences, aggressive pronouncements by outspoken leaders, and even the present peaceful demands of the Idle No More movement — suggests that the federal government has good reason to develop (or continue to develop) its intelligence collection capabilities and its public order plans and strategies as priority activities. But how aggressive should the Canadian government become?

Perhaps, in the present, increasingly uncertain circumstances, the government ought to wait to see how the situation develops and deal with particular difficulties incrementally. If the prime minister and the Cabinet understood how and why insurgencies end, assessing the third way — the waiting-to-act option — the decision to act or not to act might be easier. Fortunately, new research provides some important ways to think about how insurgencies end and what policies and tactics might encourage these endings in the government's favour.

HOW INSURGENCIES END

The 2010 Rand Corporation study *How Insurgencies End*, a comprehensive "... quantitative and qualitative analysis of 89 [insurgency] case studies ... [revealed] ... some useful insights into the relative success and failure of various methods employed by each side [insurgent and COIN] as they apply to insurgency endings."[5] The authors, Ben Connable and Martin Libicki, describe also "… the common trends of those [insurgencies] that succeed and those that fail."[6]

Four key findings emerge from the Rand Corporation research:

- Insurgent hierarchies unified in purpose and structure "do better … than do fragmented networks."
- Insurgencies rarely succeed in middle-income and urbanized countries and are best practised in rural, or a mix of rural and urban, terrain.
- Insurgencies rarely survive or succeed without some kind of sanctuary. The availability of sanctuary directly correlates with the likelihood of insurgent victory, but only if the sanctuary is provided voluntarily.
- Finally, insurgencies "… do not need to be militarily strong to win or to at least force governments to concede significant advantages to the insurgents; [indeed] … military strength can backfire." For instance, violent acts by insurgent forces may provoke a government into a sustained, armed response that the insurgents may not expect or be prepared to counter.[7]

The research on the end of insurgencies also suggests that "… insurgencies with more than two clear parties involved [i.e., additional actors beyond the government and a rebel group] have longer, more violent, and more complex endings."[8] This is because of the difficulty of trying to bring several competing parties with diverse goals to a common agreement or settlement. In such situations, it is not unusual for individual disaffected parties to break away from negotiations and continue the insurgency alone or in some new coalition.

Time, according to conventional wisdom, is usually on the side of the insurgents. The Rand study, however, found that in protracted campaigns "… over the long run, governments tend to win more often than not."[9] Interestingly, the study found, again contradicting the usual assumptions about the positive effects of outside aid, that when confronted by an insurgency, "[G]overnments benefit from direct [external] support, but tend to lose more frequently when provided with indirect [external] support; *they do slightly better with no external support at all.*"[10]

The Rand Corporation's research was intended to provide "… transferrable *end-state* indicators for intelligence professionals" which "…if properly evaluated, can help counter-insurgents recognize or create a tipping point."[11] The research suggests that the recognition of "tipping points" is the key to understanding the state of an insurgency, while creating tipping points is the key to preventing and defeating them.

A tipping point is defined as "… the point at which events take a crucial turn toward the final outcome."[12] Of course, such crucial points can favour the insurgents or they can favour the counter-insurgents. Unfortunately, whatever the case may be, such critical indicators are often difficult to identify until after the fact. Furthermore, not every insurgency has a defining tipping point, and some near-dead insurgencies have recovered after seemingly going beyond a tipping point to continue the fight. Connable and Libicki acknowledge these and other analytical difficulties and, therefore, focus their research and the considerable data they've compiled to identify and describe tipping points that clearly marked "… the beginning of the end of [a particular] insurgency."[13]

From this research, Connable and Libicki identify several "key findings" and "key indicators" that often signal "significant trends and, occasionally, tipping points." The durability and stability of an insurgency is important. "Modern insurgencies last approximately ten years and the government's chances of winning may increase slightly over time. An insurgency that hits a clear tipping point at or just before ten years typically tails out gradually to end-state at sixteen years."[14] Again, defining the absolute end of an insurgency is complicated and uncertain, but, typically, conflicts "ebb slowly rather than rapidly vanish."[15]

The authors of the study *How Insurgencies End* stress the importance of creating tipping points — for instance, encouraging desertions and defections of insurgents from operational units with bribes or safety from reprisal, or limiting the availability of a sanctuary as a central part of a counter-insurgency strategy — as an important tactic for a government. (In the Canada-First Nations context, a reserve might be considered a sanctuary). Even such basic things as prompting civilians closely connected to the insurgency to provide information to counter-insurgency forces or encouraging quiet co-operation from such individuals "may mark a shift in [operational] momentum particularly at the tactical level."[16] One of the report's key finding suggests four such strategic tipping points that might be helpful in deterring a future confrontation between Canada and the First Nations.

- **Tipping Point 1:** Discourage and disrupt the unification of any group of First Nations whose leaders advocate the use of illegal actions against Canada.
- **Tipping Point 2:** Provide significant support to individuals and families who wish to move off-reserve and into towns and cities. Support, also, the establishment of economically sound urban reserves.
- **Tipping Point 3:** Separate radical leaders from on-reserve governance and demonstrate to influential chiefs and councils the positive links between peaceful reserves that shun armed radicals and government programs that provide significant support or rewards to on-reserve people: health, education, and employment programs, for example.
- **Tipping Point 4:** Explain and demonstrate — in small numbers and in a non-threatening manner — the possible negative consequences and risks that might follow if First Nations people or bands were to openly support the use of armed force against Canada, particularly to radicals who encourage such ideas and actions.

Canadian planners and First Nations leaders, however, should heed the warning from the Rand Study that history makes clear:

> Full-blown insurgencies are messy affairs. Not one of [the Connable and Libicki] 89 cases provided an example that could be equated to an unambiguous conventional success like that of the Allies in World War II. Recent U.S. experience in COIN has

been especially tangled. Vietnam speaks for itself, as do Iraq and Afghanistan. This kind of mixed outcome is all but inevitable. However, ways exist to mitigate negative consequences. *It is possible to shape insurgency endings with sufficient forethought, strategic flexibility, and sustained willpower.* Failure to heed the past 50 years of expert opinion on the subject almost guarantees an undesirable, and possibly a disastrous, end.[17]

BUILDING A PRE-EMPTIVE "NEGOTIATE FIRST" STRATEGY

Of course, the best way "to shape insurgency endings" in Canada would be to ensure that an insurgency does not occur by anticipating events and reshaping for the greater good the negative factors that could propel Canada's peaceful society into chaos. A helpful first step in this direction would be the development of what might be called a federal government-First Nations *pre-emptive negotiating strategy* aimed at shaping future outcomes through policies designed specifically to forestall an insurgency. Unfortunately, an important step such as this is unlikely today because of inflexible ideas and "winner-takes-all" politics. As difficult to overturn such patterns as it may be, change is absolutely necessary if Canadian and First Nations leaders are to try to build a better relationship on the platform of First Nations historic grievances and non-Aboriginal Canadian social prejudices that exist today.

Interestingly, theories about insurgencies and how to prevent and defeat them can aid such negotiations for change, especially if they are used to inform the practical ways and means to shape outcomes. It's important to acknowledge, nevertheless, that transferring theory into real situations is never easy or clear-cut. Successfully pre-empting a domestic conflict through negotiations — disarming the time bomb — will depend on the political and security realities when negotiations begin. That is to say, if negotiations begin in a positive, still-peaceful atmosphere, the chance of success will be greater than if they begin after violent actions by one or both sides have already soured relationships. It is difficult at present to define precisely where the Canada-First Nations situation is on this type of spectrum. Though things are peaceful, for the most part, there have been instances of violent confrontation, and there is an increasing radicalization of the First Nations community. Building a national strategy to pre-empt an insurgency and to shape a new, safer relationship will, without doubt, demand overlapping measures to redress grievances, incremental plans to reduce enabling feasibilities, fair-minded concessions by Canada and the First Nations, and, of course, time.

BUILDING A NEGOTIATING PROCESS

The history of the resolution of internal confrontations in other locales suggests that direct negotiations between the contending parties held in quiet circumstances unencumbered by "pre-negotiation conditions" and led by delegates empowered to reach meaningful agreements are most likely to shape positive future relationships.

Carefully guarded pre-convention discussions amongst senior government officials — but not, initially, federal politicians — and some assembly of First Nations chiefs would certainly be necessary before substantive negotiations could begin. These internal government discussions would, among other things, design negotiation protocols, confirm the main issues to be discussed, set an agenda, develop a program for outreach activities meant to engage the public in the process, and develop shared administrative structures to support negotiations.

Statements regarding issues and agreements on negotiating protocols are the first steps necessary and are, probably, the easiest steps in resolving disputes. The challenge for Canadian and First Nations negotiators resides in the complexity of their (mostly) very different self-interests. For each side, the most critical issue, the heart of any serious negotiations, is its pre-conceived, deep-seated idea (likely not initially exposed to the other side) about what an acceptable final outcome would be. Whatever that vision might be, it is almost inevitable, however, that success will depend on the willingness of negotiators to discover, issue-by-issue, tolerable compromises, or, at least, mutually acceptable resolutions of contentious matters.

Despite the value of beginning bilateral discussions without pre-conditions, both Canadian and First Nations political leaders will certainly set their own boundaries around what may be negotiated and what compromises might be allowed before these negotiations begin. Anticipating before negotiations begin the other side's pre-conditions and the degree of flexibility available to its negotiators is a vitally important part of any negotiation strategy. These are not easy tasks and miscalculations can have serious negative consequences, as the federal government's shocked astonishment at the First

Nations near-total rejection of its First Nations Control of First Nations Education Act demonstrated dramatically in May 2014. As things stand now, however, it is possible to discern from various leaders' public statements and from other sources the critical issues and policy positions each side would likely bring to a negotiating table and what pre-negotiation conditions would accompany them.

FRAMEWORK FOR NEGOTIATIONS: THE FEDERAL GOVERNMENT AGENDA

The essence of Canada's strategy is to create through negotiations agreements that will pre-empt an armed or unarmed First Nations insurgency. Although the federal government's opening statements at these imagined negotiations might suggest that it believes that the road to peace can be constructed by redressing outstanding First Nations grievances, eventually its actual strategic aim, to significantly impair the feasibility of a First Nations uprising, will become apparent.

To these ends, government negotiators will defend their positions by leaning hard on "the merits of clarity," that is, on the power of a clear message, consistently delivered, and by establishing the certainty that the government's key objectives and concepts are not to be taken as mere debating points. The government would present to the conference an eight-point plan. These negotiator's guidelines would also include the government's confidential "guidance" for each item, describing carefully the boundaries beyond which negotiators would not venture without specific instructions from ministers.

❖

The principal objective of a federal government delegation to a conference to reconcile Canada and First Nations interests is to do so without surrendering or narrowing the sovereignty of Canada in any respect.

Negotiators' Guidance:
The Government of Canada recognizes the inherent right of self-government as an existing right under Section 35 of the Constitution Act, 1982, a position established as government policy and explained in detail in *The Government of Canada's Approach to Implementation of the Inherent Right and the Negotiation of Aboriginal Self-Government.* The policy explicitly sets Canada's sovereignty apart from the subordinate concept of Aboriginal self-government. The government in that document has unconditionally established the national and international boundaries of the Canadian and First Nations relationship and thereby will not join any negotiations concerning fundamental governance.

The second major federal goal is to prevent or limit the political unification of the First Nations or of a significant number of First Nations.

Negotiators' Guidance:
Dividing insurgents, and in this case the First Nations, from each other is a key tipping point in COIN theory and a major objective in the government's overall strategy. It is an objective consistent with government's responses to past First Nations disruptions, for instance, at Oka and,

later, Caledonia, where open and clandestine actions were taken to ensure that these local confrontations did not spread spontaneously to other First Nations communities or, worse, far and wide across the country.[18] Although in other circumstances prime ministers and public servants might have suggested that they would value opportunities to work with some form of Native collective, helping to create a unified and empowered Indian authority would obviously be detrimental to the federal cause.

The Government of Canada assumes that Canada-First Nations affairs and negotiations are limited nation-to-nation undertakings separate and distinct from any dealings with so-called national and/or regional First Nations assemblies.

Negotiators' Guidance:
Taking advantage of schisms, creating a tipping point within the First Nations ranks may be easier to achieve than some inside and outside those communities might admit. As with most parts of Canada's society, individual First Nations and groups of bands have particular self-interests and unique ambitions. One might expect the gulf between these separate interests to widen as economic fortunes begin to favour some communities over others. That divide is already evident as the natural resources boom in the North and West creates winners and also-rans across the Aboriginal community, and, again, in the aftermath of the FNCFNE Act, when many First Nations rejected the bill while many others did not.

The government, acting within the Canadian Constitution, would attempt during negotiations to exploit these internal divisions by declaring its intention — depending on the matter under discussion — to conduct future negotiations through limited one-on-one conversations with individual First Nations, especially if collective negotiations appear likely to disadvantage Canada.

The First Nations might have a very difficult time negotiating against a government that puts this clear intention on the table. It is, however, a difficulty of their own making. For more than twenty-five years the First Nations have styled themselves as "nations" and the federal government has generally accepted that term in its dealing with the community and with individual bands. Governments routinely accept the Assembly of First Nations as an organization that represents the individual chiefs of the First Nations as equal and independent leaders and representatives of their independent First Nations — independent, that is, from all the other First Nations and any First Nations collective organization.

By their own choice, the leaders of the First Nations decided long ago that "by virtue of [their own] recognition and respect for their mutual sovereign equality" the chiefs alone speak for the members of their respective communities.[19] Likewise, although some First Nations have organized themselves into regional associations, for instance as members of the Southern [Manitoba] Chiefs Organization or the Federation of Saskatchewan Indian Nations, the independence of each nation within such assemblies is not surrendered.

There is no such thing as a "united nations" of the First Nations of Canada and First Nations leaders insist in their dealing with the Canadian government that their communities be recognized as independent political entities. This reality was demonstrated dramatically during the so-called hunger strike mini-crisis involving Chief Theresa Spence in January 2013. Prime Minister Harper attempted to reach an agreement to settle the dispute by convening a short, restricted meeting with the national chief of the AFN and a small group of First Nations "representatives." Atleo's acquiescence to the demand to exclude other chiefs (who, coincidentally, were in Ottawa at the time) from the discussions created an uproar.

According to Atleo's sometimes rival, Professor Pam Palmater, Atleo's acceptance of the invitation to meet with the prime minister "... undercut the validity of the AFN" by disrespecting the authority of the chiefs. She criticized Atleo, who, in her opinion, should not have met with the prime minister without all of the chiefs "because [Atleo] has no independent political authority [to act alone]."[20]

Speaking to the media during the Chief Spence fracas, Professor Taiaiake Alfred, an outspoken advocate for the First Nations sovereignty, described the treaty-based relationship between Canada and Aboriginals as "nation-to-nation" and emphasized that "[T]he treaties that we're fighting so hard to have recognized and respected are treaties between nations."[21] The government, therefore, may, without risk, choose to establish and administer policies with the First Nations in a manner that these self-declared nations seem to demand; that is, in nation-to-nation discussions and negotiations.

Federal negotiators will insist that the prime minister of Canada is not obliged to deal collectively with all 617 First Nations whenever the government of Canada discusses Canada's Aboriginal policies — a prerogative supported by the Constitution of Canada and by the First Nations' insistence that they are independent entities. Current treaties, too, assume the independence of the chiefs and council in each nation, and current and new land claims and other settlements will very likely carry this concept forward into new treaties.

The government's object to degrade the feasibility of a First Nations conflict will be met principally through improvements in First Nations education, but, importantly, such education programs will be designed — as are provincial programs — to prepare students to live and work in Canada's modern democratic society and its sophisticated economy.[22]

Negotiators' Guidance:
The government appreciates the special need to work together with the First Nations to develop programs that reflect the histories, cultures, and traditions of the numerous First Nations. On the other hand, the government's overriding educational goal is to develop "better outcomes for First Nations students."[23] So-called "land-based traditional teachings," demanded by leaders such as Manitoba Chief Derek Nepinak, may very well prepare young people to live on-reserve, but what else would such an education prepare them to achieve in the decades to come?

Negotiators' Guidance:
This policy is a key concept in the government's strategy to minimize the feasibility of a First Nations uprising. As a first step in this direction, the government tabled in the

House of Commons on April 10, 2014, The First Nations Control of First Nations Educations Act (Bill C-33), an act to amend First Nations education policies.[24] The new bill was developed by the government to address the shortcomings in earlier draft proposals meant to support primary and secondary education in the First Nations community, drafts that had been rejected by the First Nations. The revised education act, constructed after consultations with First Nations leaders, "reflect[ed] the five conditions outline[d] in the November 2013 Open Letter" that Assembly of First Nations national chief Shawn Atleo sent to Ottawa.[25] Under its provisions, more than a billion dollars would be provided over three years to overhaul student education on-reserve and to provide other benefits and resources. Shawn Atleo welcomed and, with some technical reservations, seemed to endorse the revised policy.[26]

Unfortunately, the act was immediately rejected by some influential First Nations leaders. Assembly of First Nations regional chief for Quebec and Labrador, Ghislain Picard, according to media reports, complained angrily that the "... proposed bill contains mostly cosmetic changes," and he said he would challenge the government in Federal Court. The vice-chief of the Federation of Saskatchewan Indian Nations likewise attacked the minister for ignoring what he called "treaty rights."[27] The chiefs' grievances are based not on the details of the government's proposed bill or on the adequacy of the significant benefits it might bring to First Nations children, but on their opinions that the government had not properly consulted the First Nations. Others condemned the proposed legislation outright. Manitoba chief Derek Nepinak, for example, sees the new act as nothing but a continuation of governments' "… assimilation agenda" based on "… discrimination and claims to racial superiority…."[28]

As the turmoil created by the Education Act escalated, Chief Nepanik and others made threats of violence and economic blockades.[29] The government stated that Canadians do not appreciate in this or any other context threats of violence and economic blockades and advised the radical leaders to cool their rhetoric. In the end, though, the government backed down in the face of the opposition, withdrawing its bill. Atleo, under pressure from some influential chiefs, abruptly resigned as national chief. Thus, a reasonable policy negotiated with Chief Atleo and others leaders has been effectively scuttled, and the education of children on-reserve, an urgent concern, not just for First Nations but for the whole country, must now wait in line behind recycled grievances. The rejection, according to Grand Chief Kelly of British Columbia, went against the chiefs' December 2013 resolution that unanimously supported [the bill] in principle. "What government," he asked in anger, "would deal with it [the AFN]? We don't have any credibility, so that's a serious problem. We damaged our own credibility as an advocacy organizations because of lack of discipline."[30]

Under a one-on-one regime, the government could simply assume that individual protesting chiefs intend to opt out of the new program and the government, and therefore would not try to convince them to do otherwise. The government would, however, agree to turn its full attention and resources towards those Nations that do see advantages for their young people in the new plan, and would, as they agreed to join the program, begin detailed one-on-one negotiations with them to bring the promises of the new legislation into being.

The Government of Canada will increase the security guarantee in First Nations communities in order to safeguard the people and to eradicate Aboriginal criminal gangs on- and off-reserve.

> *Negotiators' Guidance:*
> The Canadian government's expectation is that First Nations leaders in nation-to-nation negotiations will support this objective so long as it is not perceived by them as another federal police agency meant to enforce government policies (the Indian Act, for instance) on First Nations' territories. The security guarantee could be enhanced through a co-operative program to create and maintain a highly qualified, national Aboriginal police force, which would be supported mainly by the federal government.

The Government of Canada will enhance its new First Nations education policy by encouraging and funding directly qualified First Nations students wishing to attend post-secondary university programs and community colleges and to subsequently profit from and contribute to Canada's economy.

The government will develop and fund, with the co-operation of willing First Nations, community-based Aboriginal health and wellness programs, on the condition that chiefs and other community leaders actively support and manage drug and alcohol abuse programs, along with programs to improve children's, women's, and elder's health care.

The government, in the interest of due diligence and open governance, insists that these negotiations confirm the right of the Government of Canada to examine the financial records and program files of any treaty and/or non-treaty First Nations activity funded by the Government of Canada. Without such creditable assurances, gaining the understanding and willing support of Canadians will be difficult, and without such support few programs would be sustainable.

FRAMEWORK FOR NEGOTIATIONS:
THE FIRST NATIONS AGENDA

Defining even tentatively the agenda of a First Nations collective is complicated by the reality that the First Nations are not a unified community with an identifiable leader or a central government. The national chief of the Assembly of First Nations, as explained earlier, is the collective public voice of the opinions, policy aims, and aspirations of First Nations chiefs and councils. Although the First Nations share many common grievances and demands with regard to restitution for injuries inflicted on their people by "the immigrants," the voice of the community, unfortunately for most Canadians, is difficult to hear in the blur of confusing messages originating in the First Nations.

That said, a First Nations agenda at any federal-First Nations convention convened to develop a strategy to pre-empt a conflict between Canada and the First Nations would be generally predictable, simply because the First Nations common message over many years has been clear and con-sistent, notwithstanding the distraction at times, when 617 voices speak from different scripts.

As predictable as are the demands, so, too, are the longstand-ing First Nations warnings that will overshadow these negoti-ations. In 2007, then–National Chief Phil Fontaine declared, "We the people have a right to be frustrated, concerned and angry and that anger is growing."[31] Six years later, in yet another tense, angry situation, Chief Wallace Fox warned Canadians that the anger in the community had not abated; rather, he said, the actions (or is it inactions?) of the government had bred within the community a new, confident militancy: "If we have to shut down the economy," he said, "then we will."[32] Fox's warning is no idle bluff. It is an entirely feasible possibility and, of course, theoretically, if it's feasible it will occur!

In an imagined national summit aimed at pre-empting an internal security emergency, the First Nations chiefs should be expected to negotiate — sometimes openly and sometimes indirectly — within the following conceptual framework.

THE PRIME DIRECTIVE

"The Creator has given us the right to govern ourselves and the right of self-determination … [these] rights and responsibilities … cannot be altered or take away by any other nation."

— *Charter of the First Nations*

- Canada must base its relationship with the First Nations on inherent and treaty rights, end unilateral decisions by governments, and affirm the government-to-government, nation-to-nation relationship between Canada and our nations.
- The First Nations will never settle for anything that compromise our rights, treaties, or principles.
- The First Nations reject absolutely Canada's efforts to unilaterally amend the Indian Act — one of the many direct attacks on our nations, including efforts to silence our languages, eliminate our culture, and dispose of our land.
- First Nations rights and responsibilities demand that we be full partners in discussions about mineral and other natural resource exploration. Ownership of such resources and participation in the exploitation of such resources are vital to the long-term sustainability of our environments, our communities, and our futures.
- Today, proud First Nations celebrate our strong voice of empowerment, which is based on our people's knowledge, languages, and traditions, and an abiding respect for the environment, trade, and alliances of governing systems that respect the rights of all. We have pushed away once and for all the failed attempts at assimilation and the outrageous denial of the existence and rights of indigenous people.

JUSTICE MURRAY SINCLAIR

- "In any discussions, Canadians must acknowledge and accept that the so-called 'First Nations problem in Canada' is not, in fact a First Nations problem, it is a Canadian problem."

- Canada and the First Nations will jointly develop and appoint a national treaties commissioner to adjudicate any disputes that may arise between the Government of Canada and any First Nation. The commissioner will report directly to the Crown.

CHIEF DEREK NEPINAK

- "The First Nations have inherent and treaty rights of self-determination and self-government recognized under international law but blatantly denied in Canada."
- The federal government must surrender to the First Nations absolute control of federally funded — at a level equivalent to provincial funding — secondary school education.

CHIEF PERRY BELLEGARDE

- "We have to be involved in the economy — fully and no longer marginalized — because if we keep talking about self-determination as indigenous peoples, that [must] be linked to self-sufficiency."

COMMUNITY NON-NEGOTIABLE DEMANDS

- The First Nations people reject and will resist with means appropriate to the situation any attempt by Canada to assimilate the people into the Canadian society.
- In these and in any future negotiations, the federal government must respect the Nations' inherent right of self-government and frame its proposals so as to respect the Nations' heritages, cultures, and traditions.

- Negotiations and every future policy conversation must be conducted on the understanding that the Nations would be entitled to the full disclosure of federal government positions under "the duty to consult" provisions of the Canadian Constitution.
- The First Nations expect the Government of Canada to adhere to a negotiated, fixed timetable for the settlement of all outstanding land claims, specific claims, and Treaty Land Entitlements agreements.
- In any future programs, funding arrangements, or settlements — for example, for specific grievances — the status quo policies governing First Nations taxation exemptions must be respected.
- The federal government must agree to fund a comprehensive First Nations medical services program equivalent to provincially funded programs. The program would be developed and supervised by a First Nations council.
- The current First Nations Policing Program must be significantly enhanced in terms of units, police officers, training, and authority. The federal government will fund this program, which will be directed by a First Nations council.

THE WHITE KNIGHT COMETH? NATURAL RESOURCES AND A NEW CANADIAN-FIRST NATIONS REALITY

The First Nations inherent right of self-government is, in 2014, still in many respects new terrain for Canada, the provinces and territories, and the First Nations. It is a creature that was resurrected in the social and legal circumstances of the 1970s and 1980s when, to be frank, most Canadians knew little about the First Nations and few politicians cared much about the so-called "Indian problem" beyond asking how they might make it go away. How things have changed in just thirty years.

The federal government has acted on occasion in the past to redress longstanding Treaty Land Entitlements and "specific claims." It may have done so out of a sense of honour, or to follow the suggestions and rulings of the Supreme Court, or, perhaps, it was the realization, as people say, "that money talks" that changed the game. Today, across Canada, the First Nations, who control by treaty much of the land filled with valuable natural resources as well as access to it, have a voice, too, and governments have clearly heard it.

In 2014, and increasingly in the coming years, many First Nations leaders and communities will be major players in deciding Canada's economic future. In two seminal papers, Brian Lee Crowley and Ken Coates, associates of the Macdonald-Laurier Institute, described the opportunities and the challenges of this new era:

> Canada finds itself today in the midst of one of the most important resources development booms in national history. The scale and intensity of resources development in Canada has kept the national economy strong in the midst of global difficulties; equally important, the vast treasure trove of Canadian resources provides solid assurance that the Canadian economy will remain

robust well into the future. These exciting
and important opportunities, however, hinge
on Canada's ability to establish fair, clear, and
durable agreements with the First Nations.[33]

As Crowley and Coates explain, establishing "durable agreements" is not a someday idea, it is, in 2014, an objective of everyday concern to the government and to the resources industries. They point to "the hotly debated" economically critical Northern Gateway project, intended to carry Alberta oil through British Columbia to Asian markets, as but one enterprise "standing at the intersection … [of] the present and future of Aboriginal/non-Aboriginal relations in Canada." This project and how Canada and First Nations interests are accommodated, they say, "… is a test of our national economy, and this is especially true with respect to the newly legally empowered First Nations communities on whose support the success of the Northern Gateway may hang."[34]

Failing this test in Canada-First Nations relations — getting it wrong — by attempting to move natural resources projects forward will have definite negative implications: "without the enthusiastic and committed support and participation of affected First Nations, the chances of the project's success plummet."[35] The reality, unrealized in most Canadian homes and businesses and by some governments and political parties, is that attempting to build Canada and its economy today and in the future "without committed support and participation of affected First Nations" could cause Canada's future success to plummet entirely.

But even with the enthusiastic and committed support of the First Nations, will a national strategy built on engaging and sharing natural resources be as invincible a "white knight" as some might expect? Perhaps the "damsel in distress" in this case is incapable of profiting from her rescue. The answer depends on what the federal government, the ten provinces, the three territories, a number of vast national and international businesses interests, and scores of First Nations large and small eventually concoct.

Behind the curtain of rights-based ownership pronouncements on the part of First Nations leaders stands a blunt "... dollars and cents reality of who gets to pocket the benefits from Canada, mining and petroleum riches."[36] Some suggest that shared benefits from the billions of natural resources dollars expected to flow into Canada in the next decade will fundamentally improve the education, health, and welfare of First Nations individuals, families, and communities. Others are not so sure.

Frances Widdowson argues that "... more Aboriginal participation in the exploitation of natural resources will not be the panacea for Aboriginal ills." It may, she admits, be beneficial for some Aboriginal people, but "infusions of cash" do not necessarily result in observable Aboriginal social development. Rather, in such situations, money, in general, is transferred not to the people but to "powerful community members and their associates."[37] If this history is played out in this new reality, then perhaps in the end we will all return to where we started.

Transforming the hope generated by natural resources riches into a bountiful new reality for the First Nations is certainly possible. It is, however, the present reality that may thwart this distant hope. The development of these vast resources will take time. Simply confirming their value, settling rights and claims, obtaining permits from governments, finding financial backing, and building infrastructure to access these mostly remote sites, will in most every case take years of quarrelsome effort. The much-heralded Northern-Ontario "Ring of Fire" project, for instance, predicted by most everyone as a flagship for future northern resource development in 2014, was suddenly stalled and then went silent as financial support for it petered out.

If benefits are to flow from resource development to the First Nations then "framework agreements," meant to guide any final settlements with resource companies, will need to be negotiated first, and that might take considerable time. Once communities and miners agree to such a framework agreement, more time, perhaps years, may be needed to reach a final settlement. And until the bottom line is signed, uncertainty will hover over every aspect of these natural resources projects.

The assumption that wealth created from natural resources will benefit the people of the First Nations needs close examination. Certainly, the resources are there, and extracting and, perhaps, refining them and moving them to market will provide some people with jobs and income. Who that might be is an open question. If it is to be Native people, then an enormous effort will be needed, *before the project begins*, to create a skilled First Nations work force. Otherwise, the work and benefits will flow to "outsiders," creating, predictably, another level of grievances in some First Nations communities.

Some First Nations people may not be especially interested in working directly or indirectly in the resource industries. They may, instead, be content to accept the long-term financial benefits they expect to come to their bands from negotiations and continue to live a traditional life. First Nations chiefs and councils are certainly capable of managing the perhaps significant funds that might come from natural resources. Managing the sometimes severely negative social effects that descend on suddenly rich communities — and not just First Nations communities — is another worry.

No matter the choices made by individual First Nations, they and the rest of Canada face two unanswered questions today. What are the First Nations and Canada to do about the current urgent issues and problems facing the people while they wait for the benefits of the natural resources boom to arrive? What are the First Nations and Canada in the coming decades to do to redress the serious problems facing scores, maybe hundreds, of First Nations that, unfortunately for them, have no recoverable natural resources in their backyards?

In the context of this essay, the lingering question is this: Will the expected flow of natural resources riches that are predicted to arrive in First Nations territory speed up, impede, or have no effect at all on the tick, tick, ticking of the time bomb in the room? It seems evident from the barriers and conditions being erected by some leaders that the boom (in resources) may produce a bountiful future for some. It could also merely provide a new stage upon which some First Nations — the natural resources winners — will act out the stale story of intra-community inequality as the First Nations losers simply wither away.

BUILDING A COHERENT CANADA-FIRST NATIONS NATIONAL SECURITY STRATEGY

What Canadian and First Nations leaders need to understand is that our inseparably linked societies are vulnerable to a violent confrontation if the time bomb in our future is not defused. Thus, discovering how the feasibility time bomb can be safely and effectively disarmed and deciding to act on that information are Canada's most pressing national challenges.

Averting this danger is made difficult not simply because of the misunderstandings that exist between non-Aboriginal and First Nations communities and the rancorous tirades these misunderstandings elicit from the leaders in both communities. Finding a safe way forward is also complicated by the complexity of modern insurgencies and by the absence in government, in the security establishments, in the media, in many cases in the academy, and, certainly, within the communities on both sides, of any clear understanding of the nature of insurgencies. What passes — even in many branches of the Canadian Armed Forces — for insurgency doctrine is mostly simplistic, unexamined policy that is almost totally useless in the circumstances Canada and the First Nations face in 2014.

A national strategy to prevent and, if necessary, disarm a First Nations insurgency that could take place in Canada's future requires the development of a sophisticated strategy, one developed from credible research in several related areas. For many years, Canadian political, military, and security strategists have used the "greed and grievance" thesis to explain the cause of insurgencies. Where, however, the cause is not either of these two villains, the counter-insurgency strategies devised by civil and military planners on behalf of their political masters are ineffective. As a result, societies are endangered.

The feasibility thesis developed over the last dozen years offers a credible conceptual framework through which governments can credibly link cause and effect by measuring identifiable insurgency "determinants." The suggestion in this book is that this theoretical approach provides a particularly helpful aid for assessing the possibility of a First Nations uprising in Canada and a guide to deterring such a possibility altogether.

Yet, a national insurgency prevention and defence strategy built solely on understanding causation would be incomplete, and, therefore, flawed — perhaps dangerously so. Strategists and security planners need to understand how and why insurgencies fail and collapse or simply fade away. Such understandings provide governments and counter-insurgency commanders with focused targets for COIN operations. Certainly, each insurgency has its own character, and most evolve over time in respect to particular circumstances. Nevertheless, modern research and recent experiences prove the value of studies that identify not only why insurgencies fail, but, most importantly, how particular COIN policies, strategies, and tactics can prompt such failures. Again, the value of this research to Canadian policy and security planners is immensely important and suggests approaches governments might take "… to shape insurgency endings" to the benefit of both Canadians and First Nations people.

Suppose that some significant event, or just common sense, convinced Canadian and First Nations leaders that their people faced dangerous times and at the same time caused these insightful leaders to acknowledge that these dangers could only be averted by a council composed of leaders from both camps who were keen to safekeep the nation. What would they discuss? The answer, despite what may seem obvious to many citizens on both sides, clearly does not seem obvious to most of the leaders who represent the government and the Native peoples of Canada. Yet, finding solutions for most of the central issues in Canada's non-Aboriginal-First Nations relationship, addressing the "determinants" that might give rise to violent insurgency, is, though complicated, likely within the reach of sincere people brainy enough to sweep the peripherals off the table so that they can speak to essential matters.

However, academics, single-issue citizens, and special-interest leaders fill the air with incoherent noise. The same is true of most government representatives and Native leaders. Strangely, no one in government or in the Assembly of First Nations seems to think it useful, before they sit down together and fill the air with rhetoric about all the problems, big and small, significant and insignificant, to construct an agenda that sets out what exactly might be discussed, why, and in what order of importance. They might, in doing so, discover the particular issues in need of urgent care and how best they might address them by acting together.

There are opportunities for Canada to improve immensely the welfare and well-being of all citizens — the wealth generated by the natural resources boom of this decade provides just one of them. It is unlikely, sadly, that the benefits of these opportunities will be realized. Canada is a country convulsed by insecurity and hesitant leadership, unwilling or unable to make the hard decisions to ensure that the country and its people — Native and non-Native — enjoy the benefits of the nation's promise. Perhaps leaving things to chance will make everything right and everyone happy. It's a strategy, but not one that has succeeded very often.

EPILOGUE

"After generations of injustice and mistreatment the
First Nations people deserve their own homeland and
the right to live peacefully in that homeland."

— *Anonymous*

Time Bomb argues that a nationwide First Nations insurgency is feasible and, therefore, according to theory, inevitable. The image of a First Nations time bomb ticking away somewhere in Canada's future, however, is meant to suggest also a looming national danger that will exist and grow *only so long as the major determinants of such an insurgency are left unattended.* No one knows how much time remains on the bomb's detonating mechanism, but no one today should dismiss the presence of that bomb or underestimate the damage it could inflict on Canada, on its vulnerable economy and international reputation, and, most importantly, on its population, both non-Aboriginal and First Nations, if it explodes.

The presence of "the determinants" that have created in Canada an uprising feasibility have been described in this essay and demonstrated practically by First Nations leaders in demonstrations and periodic uprisings across the land over the last few years. Impressive First Nations leaders, people such as George Maneul, David Ahenwkew, George Erasmus, Ovide Mercredi, Phil Fontaine, and Shawn Atleo (recently overthrown by more radical modern leaders), have consistently warned and continue to warn that the status quo cannot be maintained. Policies that create destitute Native communities, with sub-standard health and education conditions, must be changed; the unfair application of the law, resulting in prisons filled with Native youth, must be ended; and most grating, Canada's continuing failure to settle honourably and appropriately outstanding land claims issue must be corrected. Too often, however, newer leaders and their more combative arguments are received by Canadians as hostile, irresponsible, rabble-rousing demagoguery. And so they walk away unconvinced and disgruntled.

Canadian political leaders, perhaps with the exception of Prime Minister Paul Martin at Kelowna in 2005, continue to argue from and act on the premise that Canada's sovereignty is indivisible and that the subordination of Aboriginal people (with or without treaties) to the policies of the federal government is reasonable and just. Politicians point to their responsibility to manage the nation's business according to law and established parliamentary practice. Protecting the public purse and accounting for public expenditures — though from time to time the government's actions in this regard are a scandal in Canada — is also a central principal of parliamentary practice. Thus, managing and accounting for expenditures and funds directed to Aboriginal people is, ultimately, a responsibility of the government. As a result of this financial imbalance in the relationship, the First Nations are necessarily subordinate to the Canadian government.

This situation and the notion behind it infuriates many present-day chiefs, who claim that the funds are the right of the First Nations and that they, as sovereign entities, cannot be held to account by Canada's Parliament. In discussions between the government and First Nations, however, the principal dispute, as with many other issues, is soon swallowed whole by esoteric arguments over degrees of sovereignty and thus forgotten. The pattern played itself out in classic form with the government's introduction in 2014 of the First Nations Control of First Nations Education Act. The act was immediately rejected by most of the more powerful chiefs in Canada, not because of the fundamentals of the act, but because of the manner in which the act was constructed and introduced.

Such issues and actions continually confound Canada–First Nations relations. However, amongst the irritants that sour this relationship the Indian Act stands without peer. It is to both cohorts of leaders the most despised, but, at the same time, the most essential act of Parliament governing Canadian-First Nations relations. As Chief Harold Cardinal explained in 1969: "We don't want the Indian Act ... but it is a lever in our hands and an embarrassment to the government." Leaders in both communities cannot, it seems, do without the act — or at least many of its central dictates. Neither can they agree, however, to amend the act in any way suited to modern circumstances. The time bomb is energized by this impediment in the broad sense that it is a grievance/conflict-producing instrument. Ironically, although the act was created to give the government the tools to oversee Canada's Aboriginal people, the Indian Act today provides to the First Nations a handy stick with which to beat hapless governments.

We, the two communities, are akin to an old, long-divorced couple, resentful of each other, who unchangeable circumstance has decreed must continue to live together in the same house forever. The arguments from both sides travel in circles. Long-past grievances linger, providing ready ammunition to fire during present-day disputes. Antique household artifacts — the Royal Proclamation of 1773, the source of both the rights and privileges acquired more than a century later and the Indian Act — cannot be moved or even refurbished for the benefit of the young or the nation. There is no ground for compromise. All such ideas and suggestions smack of surrender and betrayal to both parties. Elders who speak of reasonable accommodation are met by both parties with suspicion and contrived objections. Weapons, seldom used, stand ready in dark closets. Perhaps in these circumstances it would be best to burn the house to the ground!

It's a preposterous idea, of course. Or is it? Consider the long bloody rebellions in Ireland, where crimes against humanity were ignited by disputes over sovereignty on a tiny island. Recall also the costs in lives, the gruesome murder of young men and boys, and the destruction of entire towns and economies during the insurgencies and counter-attacks during the Balkans civil wars (1991–2001). The present-day wars of attrition, General Smith's "wars among the people," across the Middle East and along the embattled southern shores of the Mediterranean Sea are, by most modern standards, vicious insanities propelled by irrational ideas and radical leaders. No one should underestimate the power of cynicism, prejudice, and tales, real or invented, of rights denied and riches stolen to send people into the night to kill their neighbours and hang small children from their backyard swings.

These are wars launched not in search of territory, or riches, or security. Rather, they are murderous wars propelled by fundamentalist ideas against which there is no defence but counterattack. But, you will say, not in Canada, "the country that works." Certainly Molly Grace, the mythical revolutionary First Nations leader from the novel *Uprising*, won't actually appear in Canada, will she?

The leaders in both non-Aboriginal Canada and in First Nations communities are obliged to refashion the relationship between the two sides in a manner that will draw citizens away from the allure of a "we win, you lose" mentality, and its offspring: insurgency and counter-insurgency. First Nations chiefs need to disavow other Native leaders who declare, for instance, "There are only two ways of dealing with the white man. Either you pick up a gun or you stand between him and his money."[1] On the other hand, Canadian citizens and their leaders must acknowledge that they owe a duty to the Aboriginal people in Canada, a duty to listen without prejudice to their stories and to help them as they decide to redress and rebuild their societies and communities to the healthy, prosperous, and safe standards expected in the rest of the country.

The road to this new relationship must be built on the foundations of reasonable accommodation of the values, traditions, and community interests of both sides. Harsh language, threatening statements, and waving fists are behaviours that create the murderous circumstances that benefit the frightful leaders who command the bloody insurrections Canadians see every day in the evening news. Conversations, on the other hand, that begin with sincere pledges to "develop policies and agreements that respect our cultures and ensures that Canada as a country remains united and safe with fair benefits for all" might actually lead us to a country that does work.

That period of peace and reconciliation will never arrive if Canadian and First Nations leaders continue to behave and act as self-centred advocates who think that relations constructed on a platform of threats serve as the way to peace and well-being for future generations. If Canadians doubt the frightful power of zealots and combative groups — ethnic, political, and religious — who will use any means necessary, including destroying an economy and creating in city streets huge mounds of bloody corpses, to advance their demands, they certainly haven't been paying attention to the realities of the twenty-first century. Nor have they been paying attention to the radical leaders in the First Nations and the counter-radicals in the streets in Canada.

"Never in Canada" you say. Perhaps.

But beware, as you consider this book, that a time bomb aimed at hopeful Canadians like you is at this moment ticking away.

ACKNOWLEDGEMENTS

Several friends and colleagues made important contributions to the development of the concept underlying this study and to the preparation and publication of *Time Bomb*. Patrick Boyer, friend and scholarly adviser, first as President of Blue Butterfly Books and today as a senior associate of Dundurn Press encouraged me to write the novel *Uprising*. He did so again when I suggested a study that is now this finished work. At every stage in the evolution of these books Patrick was the ready, sure hand as I made my way through what were, in some regards, new intellectual and technical territories. Special thanks to Patrick for introducing me to the leaders and professional staff of Dundurn and for championing *Time Bomb* in their demanding presence.

Brian Lee Crowley, managing director of the Macdonald-Laurier Institute, and Professor Kenneth Coates, Canada Research Chair, University of Saskatchewan, though not directly associated with this work, have over the last several years encouraged and supported my studies of Aboriginal affairs in Canada. In May 2013, the MLI published *Canada And The First Nations: Co-operation or Conflict?* a report on my earlier research into some of the questions and themes raised in *Time Bomb*. I am happy to report that I continue to enjoy the benefits of their advice and ongoing interest in my research into the complicated story of First Nations and Canadian affairs in Canada today.

It may seem odd to some, but Chief Terry Nelson, Grand Chief of the Southern [Manitoba] Chiefs Organization — to some a radical, outspoken, and relentless champion of First Nations' sovereignty — in our several meetings and other conversations, and also through his many emails and publications and public activities over the last few years, contributed much to my understanding of what he once mentioned in passing as, "the sense of the people." That is, to the deep attachment they have to the land, to their culture and traditions, and, most especially, to the profound sadness that envelops many of the people, particularly the elders, when they recall or relate their sense of loss occasioned by their experiences with Canadians. I hope I was able to capture Chief Nelson's deep dedication to his people in this monograph.

Bonnie Butlin is a unique friend and colleague. She is a graduate of the University of Calgary (B.A. Political Science) and Carleton University (M.A. International Affairs). She is a co-founder and executive director of the Canadian Security Partners' Forum; vice-chair of the Infrastructure Security Partnership; co-chair at National Capital Security Partners' Forum; and executive director of the Canadian Association for Security and Intelligence Studies. Bonnie is personally and professionally attached to the Aboriginal community in Canada and kindly offered to read and provide comments on my draft text and to write, as well, a foreword to this work.

Dominic Farrell diligently edited this monograph and what clarity and sound structure it may have is due in no small way to his careful reviews of the work as it progressed, draft-by-draft. I appreciated Dominic's unrelenting enthusiasm for the theme and the First Nations story. Where others in his place might have been satisfied with "good enough," Dominic insisted on "as good as it can possibly be." This is the second major book that he and I have worked on together — the other being *Uprising* — and I learned important lessons about style and pace in both cases. Thanks Dominic and here's to next time.

NOTES

CHAPTER 1

1. "Aboriginal Peoples in Canada: First Nations People, Métis, and Inuit," *2011 National Household Survey,* Statistics Canada, May 13, 2013 [99-011-x]. Hereinafter, *NHS 2011.* See "First Nations" and "Table 2."

2. "Aboriginal Identity & Terminology," 2009, *http://indigenousfoundations.arts.ubc.ca.*

3. Care is advised in the use of "traditional" names as spelling and punctuation vary from one source to another.

4. Métis National Council, "Citizenship," 2014, *www.metisnation.ca/index.php/who-are-the-metis/citizenship.*

5. Canada, Aboriginal Affair and Northern Development Canada (hereinafter, AANDC),

"The Indian Register," January 2011, *www.aadnc-aandc.gc.ca/eng/1100100032475/110010 0032476.*

6. Statistics Canada, "Membership in a First Nation or Indian band," Approved April 20, 2009, modified May 08, 2013, *www.statcan.gc.ca/concepts/definitions/aboriginal-autochtone5-eng.htm.*

7. Statistics Canada, "First Nations, Métis, and Inuit Women," [89-503-X], modified May 13, 2013, *www.statcan.gc.ca/pub/89-503-x/2010001/article/11442-eng.htm.*

8. For a comprehensive, but reader-friendly history of the struggle for women's rights on-reserve see: Wayne Brown, "Mary Two-Axe Earley: Crusader for Equal Rights for

Aboriginal Women," *Electoral Insight* (November 2003).

9. Canada, Queen's Bench Winnipeg Centre, "Canadian National Railways vs Terrance Nelson, *et al.*, Brief of Responding Party Terrance Nelson," File No. CI 13-01-81569. The court challenge was subsequently dismissed.

CHAPTER 2

1. Thomas King, *The Inconvenient Indian: A Curious Account of Native Life in North America* (Canada: Doubleday Canada, 2012), 193.

2. "The Royal Proclamation, October 7, 1763," *www.Solon.org/Constitutions/Canada/English/Preconfederation/rp_1763.html.*

3. *Ibid.* The irregularly capitalized words are in the original document.

4. *Ibid.*

5. *Ibid.*

6. Brandon Morris and Jay Cassel, "'the said Lands … shall be purchased only for Us' [*sic*]: The Effect of the Royal Proclamation on Government," *History Matters* (October 2, 2013), 2, *www.activehistory.ca*. See also, Canada, AANDC, *Comprehensive Claims, www.aadnc-aandc.gc.ca/eng/1100100030577/1100100030578.*

7. Morris and Cassel, "the said Lands," 1.

8. National Chief Shawn A-in-chut Atleo, "First Nations and the Future of Canadian Citizenship," speech delivered at 11th Lafontaine-Baldwin Symposium, August 10, 2013. (Emphasis added)

9. *Ibid.*

10. Prime Minister Sir John A. Macdonald as quoted in "The Indian Act," *http://indigenousfoundations/arts.ubc.ca.* (Emphasis added).

11. Canada, Indian Act (R.S.C. 1985 c.1–5), modified December 19, 2013, *www.law-lois.justice.gc.ca.*

12. *Ibid.*, "Definitions," "A Superintendent includes a commissioner, regional supervisor, Indian superintendent, assistant Indian superintendent and any other person declared by the Minister to be a superintendent for the purposes of this Act, and with reference to a band or a reserve, means the superintendent for that band or reserve."

13. John Daschuk, *Clearing the Plains: Disease, Politics of Starvation and the Loss of Aboriginal life* (Regina: University of Regina Press), xxi.

14. See, Canada, AANDC, "Attempts to Reform or Repeal the Indian Act," modified July 07, 2013, *www.aadnc-aandc.gc.ca/eng/1323350306544/1323350388999.*

15. *Ibid.* See also, Daniel Wilson, "Repeal the Indian Act and

abolish the department of Indians Affairs," *This Magazine* (October 12, 2011).

16. Bill C-428 was reinstated in the 41st Parliament, 2nd Session. Currently, as of September 9, 2014, it is "In committee" in the Senate.

17. Kemble Consulting, "First Nations Relations: Bill C-248 Analysis and Commentary" (undated).

18. Chief Wilson-Raybould, "Speaking Notes on Bill C-428: Indian Act Amendment and Replacement Act," 2, a presentation to the House of Commons Standing Committee on Aboriginal Affairs and Northern Development, April 18, 2013. (Emphasis added).

19. Assembly of First Nations (AFN), "Assembly of First Nations National Chief Says Work to Move Beyond the Indian Act Must Be Led by First Nations," October 19, 2012, *www.afn.ca/index.php/ en/news-media/latest-news/ assembly-of-first-nations-na- tional-chief-says-work-to-move- beyond-indi.*

20. Harold Cardinal, *Unjust Society,* 2nd ed. (Vancouver: Douglas & MacIntyre, 1999), 140.

21. "The Indian Act," *http://indigi- nousfoundation.arts.ubc.ca*

22. AFN, "The Royal Proclamation, 1763–2013," *www.afn. ca/index.php/en/news-media/ current-issues/royal-proclamation.*

23. Canada, Department of Justice, "Constitutional Acts, 1867 to 1982, Part II, Section 35: Rights of the Aboriginal Peoples of Canada," *Justice Laws Website, Constitutional Documents, laws-lois.justice.gc.ca/eng/ Const/page-16.html#h-52.*

24. For a very readable summary of the duty to consult legal doctrine see, Dwight Newman, *The Rule and Role of Law: The Duty to Consult, Aboriginal Communities, and the Canadian Natural Resources Sector,* Aboriginal Canada and the Natural Resource Economy: 4 (Ottawa: Macdonald-Laurier Institute, May 2014), 8.

25. Canada, Prime Minister of Canada, First Nations Control of First Nations Education Act, February 7, 2014.

26. Canada, AANDC, "The Government of Canada's Approach to Implementation of the Inherent Right and the Negotiation of Aboriginal Self-Government: Policy Framework: Inherent Right of Self-Government is a Section 35 Right," *www. aadnc-aandc.gc.ca/eng/11001 00031843/1100100031844.* (Emphasis added.)

27. *Ibid.,* "Policy Framework: Within the Canadian Constitutional Framework." (Emphasis added.)

28. *Ibid.,* "Policy Framework: Scope of Negotiations." (Emphasis added.)

29. Canada, AANDC, "Backgrounder — Urban Reserves: A Quiet Success Story," *www.aadnc-aandc.gc.ca/eng/110010 0016331/1100100016332*.

30. *Ibid.*

31. *Ibid.*

32. Canada, AANDC, "Fact Sheet: Aboriginal Self-Government," modified August 30, 2013, *www.aadnc-aandc.gc.ca/eng/110010001 6293/1100100016294*.

33. *Ibid.*

34. Canada, AANDC, "The Government of Canada's Approach to Implementation of the Inherent Right and the Negotiation of Aboriginal Self-Government."

35. Atleo, "First Nations and the Future of Canadian Citizenship," August 10, 2013.

CHAPTER 3

1. Douglas L. Bland, *Canada and The First Nations: Cooperation or Conflict*, Aboriginal Canada and the Natural Resource Economy Series: 2 (Ottawa: Macdonald-Laurier Institute, May 2013), 11.

2. For a brilliant description of this modern evolution and its links to resource development see: Ken Coates and Brian Lee Crowley, *New Beginnings: How Canada's Natural Resource Wealth Could Re-shape Relations with Aboriginal People*, Aboriginal Canada and the Natural Resource Economy Series: 1 (Ottawa: Macdonald-Laurier Institute, May 2013).

3. Statistics Canada, "Aboriginal Peoples In Canada: First Nations, Métis, and Inuit," from *2011 National Household Survey*, [99-011-X 2011001].

4. *Ibid.*

5. Andrea Levatt, et al., "Aboriginal People in Canada in 2006: Inuit, Métis, First Nations People," *2006 Census*, Statistics Canada [97-558-X], modified June 21, 2010, *www12.statcan.gc.ca/census-recensement/2006/as-sa/97-558/p15-eng.cfm*.

6. Assembly of First Nations, "A Portrait of First Nations and Education," Paper delivered at the Chiefs Assembly on Education Conference, Gatineau, QC, October 1–3, 2012, 2. See also, Assembly of First Nations, "Fact Sheet: First Nations Post-Secondary Education," 2011, *www.afn.ca/uploads/files/pse-fact-sheet.pdf*.

7. *NHS 2011.*

8. *Ibid.*

9. *Ibid.*

10. Assembly of First Nations, "A Portrait of First Nations and Education," 3, *www.afn.ca/uploads/files/events/fact_sheet-ccoe-3.pdf*.

11. See, for instance, Gloria Galloway, "First Nations leaders split over bill regarding on-reserve education," *Globe and Mail*, April 28, 2014; Gloria Galloway, "Conservatives put

First Nations education bill 'on hold' after Atleo quits," *Globe and Mail*, May 5, 2014; "B.C. natives disavow economic threat." *National Post*, May 16, 2014.

12. "Aboriginal Statistics at A Glance," Chart 11: Median total income in 2005 by Aboriginal identity, population aged 25 to 54, *2006 Census*, Statistics Canada [89-645-X], last modified June 21, 2010, *www.statcan.gc.ca/pub/89-645-x/2010001/c-g/c-g011-eng.htm*.

13. Jeannine Usalcas, *Aboriginal People and the Labour Market: Estimates from the Labour Force Survey, 2008–2010*, Aboriginal Labour Force Series, Statistics Canada [71-588-X], last modified April 15, 2013, *www.statcan.gc.ca/pub/71-588-x/71-588-x2011003-eng.htm*.

14. Health Canada, *First Nations & Inuit Health: Diseases and Health Conditions*, December 7, 2012, *www.hc-sc.gc.ca/fniah-spnia/diseases-maladies/index-eng.php*.

15. Linda Gionet and Shirin Roshanafshar, *Health at a Glance: Current Smoking Trends*, Charts 2a and 2b, Statistics Canada [82-624-X], modified January 1, 2013, *www.statcan.gc.ca/pub/82-624-x/2012001/article/11676-eng.pdf*.

16. Health Canada, "First Nations & Inuit Health: Diseases & Health Conditions," last modified December 7, 2012, *www.hc-sc.gc.ca/fniah-spnia/diseases-maladies/index-eng.php*.

17. Public Health Agency Canada, "Diabetes in Canada: Facts and Figures from A Public Health Perspective, Report Highlights [Chapter Six]," last modified December 15, 2011, *www.phac-aspc.gc.ca/cd-mc/publications/diabetes-diabete/facts-figures-faits-chiffres-2011/highlights-saillants-eng.php*.

18. Public Health Agency Canada, "Population-Specific HIV/AIDS Status Report Aboriginal Peoples. Executive Summary," last modified September 8, 2010, *www.phac-aspc.gc.ca/aids-sida/publication/ps-pd/aboriginal-autochtones/index-eng.php*.

19. Health Canada, "First Nations & Inuit Health: Mental Health and Wellness," modified February 4, 2013, *www.hc-sc.gc.ca*.

20. *Ibid.*

21. Office of the Chief Coroner of Ontario, "Appendix 4," in *The Office of the Chief Coroner's Death Review of the Youth Suicides at the Pikangikum First Nation, 2006–2008*, *http://provincialadvocate.on.ca/documents/en/Coroners_Pik_Report.pdf*.

22. Linda Gionet and Shirin Roshanafshar, *Health at a Glance: Select Health Indicators of First Nations People Living Off Reserve, Métis, and Inuit* (Ottawa: Statistics Canada, January 2013), [82-

624-X], *www.statcan.gc.ca/
pub/82-624-x/2012001/arti-
cle/11676-eng.pdf.*

23. Office of the Chief Coroner,
Chief Coroner's Death Review.

24. Anne Milan and Covadonga
Robles, "Women in Canada:
A Gender-based Statistical
Report: Female Popula-
tion" (Aboriginal Identity),
Statistics Canada [89-503-
X], last modified May 13,
2013, *www.statcan.gc.ca/
pub/89-503-x/2010001/arti-
cle/11475-eng.htm#a5.*

25. Canada, AANDC, "Better
Outcomes for First Nations
Children: Aboriginal Affairs
and Northern Development
Canada's Role as a Funder
in First Nations Child and
Family Services," updated
May 2013, *www.aadnc-aandc.
gc.ca/eng/1100100035210/11
00100035218.*

26. Amnesty International,
"Discrimination Against First
Nations Children In Canada,"
*www.amnesty.ca/category/
issue/indigenous-peoples/in-
digenous-peoples-in-canada/
discrimination-against-first-na-
tions?type=blog.*

27. *Ibid.*

28. Canada, AANDC, "Better
Outcomes for First Nations
Children."

29. Health Council of Canada,
*Empathy, Dignity, and Respect:
Creating Cultural Safety for
Aboriginal People in Urban
Health Care* (December 2012).

30. Health Council of Canada,
*Canada's Most Vulnerable:
Improving Health Care for
First Nations, Inuit, and Métis
Seniors* (November 2013).

31. *Ibid.*

32. *Ibid.*

33. *Ibid.*

34. First Nations Information
Governance Centre, "First
Nations Regional Longitudi-
nal Health Survey: Phase 2
(2008–10)," Revised Edition,
2011, 23.

35. "Drug Abuse Major Concern
Among First Nations and
Inuit," *Aboriginal Health
News,* June 27, 2011. See
also, "High rates of injector
drug use in urban Aboriginal
youth signal need for preven-
tative programs," *Canadian
Medical Association Journal*
(CMAJ) (June 13, 2011).

36. "Crisis of Suicide, Drug
Addiction Deepens Among
Northern Ontario First
Nations." Yahoo News, *Daily
Brew,* April 18, 2013.

37. "Cat Lake: Children on First
Nations Reserve Send Heart-
breaking Letter to Drug-
Addicted Parents." *Huffington
Post:* Politics, April 15, 201.

38. "Crisis of Suicide," Yahoo News,
Daily Brew, April 18, 2013.

39. *National Post,* February 23, 2012.

40. Canada, "Aboriginal People as
Victims of Crime" *National
Victims of Crime Awareness
Week,* April 10, 2013, *www.
victimsweek.gc.ca/res/r57.html.*

41. *Ibid.,* Table 2.

42. Samuel Perreault and Tina Hotton Mahony, "Criminal Victimization In The Territories, 2009," Statistics Canada, *Juristat,* 2012, (85-002-X), *www.statcan.gc.ca/pub/85-002-x/2012001/article/11614-eng.htm.*

43. Shannon Brennan, "Violent Victimization of Aboriginal Women in the Canadian Provinces, 2009." 85-002-x, Statistics Canada, *Juristat,* 2011 (85-002-X), *www.statcan.gc.ca/pub/85-002-x/2011001/article/11439-eng.htm.* The main findings of this 2011 Statistics Canada report were recently confirmed by the RCMP in their study: *Missing and Murdered Aboriginal Women: A National Operational Overview,* May 16, 2014.

44. Raven Sinclair and Jana Grekulb, "Aboriginal Youth Gangs In Canada: (De)Constructing An Epidemic," *First People and Family Review* 7, no. 1, (2012): 9.

45. See, for example, Wanda D. McCaslin and Yvonne Boyer, "First Nations Communities at Risk And in Crisis: Justice and Security," *Journal of Aboriginal Health* (November 2009): 61–87.

46. Mark Totten. "Preventing Aboriginal Youth Gang Involvement in Canada: A Gendered Approach," a paper prepared for the Aboriginal Policy Research Conference (March 2009).

47. Mark Totten, "Aboriginal Youth and Violent Gang Involvement in Canada: Quality Prevention Strategies," *IPC Review* 3 (March 2009): 135–56.

48. Canadian Press, "Native gangs spreading across Canada," *CBC News,* March 16, 2010, *www.cbc.ca/news/canada/manitoba/native-gangs-spreading-across-canada-1.873168.*

49. "RCMP estimates 50 contraband tobacco, manufacturers operating in First Nations territories in Ontario and Quebec," *National Post,* August 27, 2013.

50. Canadian Press, "Native gangs spreading across Canada," March 16, 2010.

51. "Gangs starting to 'infect' women's prisons," *Calgary Herald,* May 25, 2012.

52. *Ibid.*

53. Canada, Office of the Correctional Investigator, "Backgrounder: Aboriginal Offenders — A Critical Situation," modified September 16, 2013, *www.oci-bec.gc.ca.*

54. *Ibid.*

55. Statistics Canada, "Adult Correctional Statistics Canada, 2010/2011," *Juristat,* (85-002-X), *www.statcan.gc.ca/pub/85-002-x/2012001/article/11715-eng.htm.*

56. The data for British Columbia and Eastern Canada were not included in this reference.

57. Douglas L. Bland, *Canada and The First Nations: Cooperation or Conflict*, Aboriginal Canada and the Natural Resource Economy Series: 2 (Ottawa: Macdonald-Laurier Institute, May 2013), 14.

CHAPTER 4

1. Paul Collier, et al., "Beyond Greed and Grievance: Feasibility and Civil War," *Oxford Economic Papers*, 61, no. 1 (January 2009): 1.
2. Rupert Smith. *The Utility of Force: The Art of War in the Modern World.* (London: Penguin Books, 2006), 3–4.
3. Paul Collier, "Ethnic Civil Wars: Securing the Post-Conflict Peace." *Harvard International Review*, 8, no. 4 (Winter 2007): 1.
4. R. Scott Moore, "The Basics of Counterinsurgency," *Small Wars Journal* (May 2007): 2. (Italics in the original)
5. To answer my own question, I will usually use insurgency to describe a First Nations' confrontation simply because the term is commonly used in the context that we will address and second, it has — for better or worse and usually for better — a useful degree nuance that will allow the term to fit into various situations to be addressed in this book.

6. James Daschuk, *Clearing the Plains: Disease, Politics of Starvation, and the Loss of Aboriginal Life* (Regina: University of Regina Press, 2013).
7. The best reference to this confrontation is: Harry Swain, *Oka: Apolitical Crisis and Its Legacy* (Vancouver: Douglas & McIntyre, 2010).
8. Ontario Justice Education Network, *Landmark Case: The Ipperwash Inquiry*, An OJEN *Courtrooms & Classrooms* Resource, *www.ojen.ca/sites/ojen.ca/files/sites/default/files/resources/Ipperwash%20Inquiry%20English.pdf.*
9. Christie Blatchford, *Helpless: Caledonia's Nightmare of Fear and Anarchy And How the Law Failed All Of Us* (Canada: Doubleday Canada, 2011).
10. *Ibid.*, 200.
11. See, for example, "First Nations Fight Against the Frackers," *Global Research*, January 06, 2014, and "Police arrest 40 at New Brunswick fracking protest," *Toronto Star*, October 17, 2013.
12. Yadullah Hussain, "Fort Mackay eyes oil sand production," *National Post*, March 14, 2014.
13. "B.C. natives disavow economic threat." *National Post*, May 16, 2014.
14. This demand takes us into the field of "essentially contested concepts," wherein, in very generally terms, the debate turns not on the object itself but on

the *contested* words and definitions claim to describe the concept: i.e "This is an insurgency. Perhaps, but that conclusion depends on your definitions of the concept, *insurgency*." But we don't need to try to untangle this difficulty in this book, but *understand*, we tend in everyday usage to resolve such essentially contested concepts by substituting some previously agreed norm to serve as the basis for defining it. For those interested in the philosophic discussion of this and related ideas, a classic argument is described by W.B. Gallie in "Meeting of the Aristotelian Society London," March 12, 1956.

15. Collier, "Ethnic Civil Wars," 2.

16. Of course, time and the ascent of new leaders with almost dictatorial powers can at most any time reverse this hopeful beginning. Some have argued that this regression may be underway, or already a *fait accompli* in South Africa today.

17. Collier, et al., "Beyond Greed and Grievance," 2.

18. *Ibid.*

19. *Ibid.*, 3.

20. *Ibid.*

21. A version of this description of feasibility factors was published in Douglas L. Bland, *Canada and The First Nations: Cooperation or Conflict*, Aboriginal Canada and the Natural Resource Economy: 2 (Ottawa: Macdonald-Laurier Institute, May 2013).

22. Collier, et al., "Beyond Greed and Grievance," 15.

23. *Ibid.*, 16.

24. *Ibid.*, 16.

25. *Ibid.*, 13.

26. *Ibid.*, 15.

27. *Ibid.*, 2.

28. *Ibid.*, 24.

CHAPTER 5

1. Douglas L. Bland, *Canada and The First Nations: Cooperation or Conflict*, Aboriginal Canada and the Natural Resource Economy: 2 (Ottawa: Macdonald-Laurier Institute, May 2013), 24.

2. This book is not an academic exercise aimed at trying to falsify the hypothesis; that is, to suggest that because a First Nations insurgency is feasible in terms of the hypothesis but has not occurred that the hypothesis is, therefore, false.

3. Consider the government's attempts to settle the Aboriginal Residential Schools issue which many Canadians might assume was "solved" when Prime Minister Harper, on behalf of all Canadians, apologized and set in place policies to compensate former residents for the mistreatments they suffer. Today, the redress/compensation process is in many respects the source of scores of new grievances.

4. Statistics Canada, "Aboriginal People in Canada, Part 2: Aboriginal Population is Young," *NHS 2011.*

5. Statistics Canada, "Ontario: Aboriginal People: Table 1," Focus on Geography, *NHS 2011*, modified April 17, 2014, *www12.statcan.gc.ca/nhs-enm/2011/as-sa/fogs-spg/Pages/Fog.cfm?lang=E&level=2&Geo-Code=35.*

6. When the Highway 17 bridge north of the village of Wawa collapsed in a flood in 2012, cross-Canada vehicle traffic was delayed for days, leaving only a long difficult detour through the United States as an option: "Highway reopened in Ontario town of Wawa after washout," *Toronto Sun*, October 30, 2012.

7. Not to be too obvious, but the principle could be read (more in keeping with the others): *The lack of a* credible security guarantee makes the risk of civil war *less* dangerous for insurgents and thus an insurgency *more* feasible.

8. Paul Collier, et al., "Beyond Greed and Grievance: Feasibility and Civil War," *Oxford Economic Papers,* 61, no. 1, (January, 2009): 15.

9. Collier's research of this determinant was developed mainly from assessments of natural resources effects on states and civil wars in underdeveloped African states. Nevertheless, the concept and findings are relevant to developed states dependant economically on natural resources.

10. Canada, Library of Parliament, "Trade and Investment 2012: Canada's Merchandise Trade with the World," June 7, 2013, (2013-29-E), *www.parl.gc.ca/Content/LOP/Research-Publications/2013-29-e.pdf.*

11. Canada, "Responsible Resource Development," *Canada's Economic Action Plan, 2013, http://actionplan.gc.ca.*

12. "Agri-business includes activities of food and fibre production and processing which are not part of the farm operation. This would include the production of farm equipment and fertilizers to aid farm production. Agribusiness also includes the firms that purchase the raw goods from the farm for further processing. The meat packing industry, flour mill, and canning industry would be included in the agribusiness sector processing farm products." "Agriculture in Canada," *Wikipedia*, 2014.

13. Canada, Agriculture and Agri-Foods Canada, "An Overview of the Canadian Agriculture and Agri-Foods System, 2013," modified May 22, 2013, *www.agr.gc.ca/eng/about-us/publications/economic-publications/alphabetical-listing/an-over-*

view-of-the-canadian-agri-culture-and-agri-food-system-2013/?id=1331319696826.

14. Canada, Transport Canada, "Transportation in Canada," *2010* (June 2011), 4, *www.tc.gc.ca/media/documents/policy/overview2010.pdf.*

15. See, for example, Douglas L. Bland, *Canada and The First Nations: Cooperation or Conflict,* Aboriginal Canada and the Natural Resource Economy: 2 (Ottawa: Macdonald-Laurier Institute, May 2013).

16. Scott Deveau, "Port may cancel truckers' permits," *National Post,* March 18, 2014.

17. Scott Deveau, "Truckers dash hope of end to port strike," *National Post,* March 17, 2014.

18. Railway Association of Canada, "Rail Facts," *www.railcan.ca/education/facts2012.*

19. Statistics Canada, "Railway Carloadings, September 2013," *www.statcan.gc.ca/daily-quotidien/131127/dq131127c-eng.pdf.*

20. Bland, *Canada and The First Nations: Cooperation or Conflict,* 29.

21. Respectively, Hydro Quebec, 2010; Ontario Hydro One, *"Quick Facts,"* 2012; and "BC Hydro 50," 2012.

22. Jon Elmer, "Canada's Brewing Insurgency," *Aljazeera.net,* June 26, 2010.

CHAPTER 6

1. Terry Nelson, "How Dangerous is the Situation In Canada?" Yahoo. com, *Daily Brew* (March 2012), quoted in "Militant AIM [*sic*] leader who visited Iran now Grand Chief of Manitoba SCO," *Red Power Media,* January 11, 2014, *http://redpowermedia.wordpress.com/.*

2. Vo Nguyên Giap, *People's War People's Army: The Viet Công Insurrection Manual for Underdeveloped Countries* (Washington: Frederick A. Praeger, 1962), xxiii–xxvii.

3. Assembly of the First Nations, "Charter of the Assembly of First Nations," August 20, 1986 (as amended), *www.afn.ca/index.php/en/about-afn/charter-of-the-assembly-of-first-nations.*

4. Atleo, "First Nations and the Future of Canadian Citizenship," August 10, 2013, 6. (Emphasis added).

5. See, for instance, Canadian reactions to First Nations disturbances in January 2013: "Fast Fallout: Chief Spence and Idle No More Movement Galvanizes Canadians Around Money Management and Accountability," *Ipsos.com,* January 15, 2013; Michael Woods, "Majority of Canadians concerned about financial accountability on First Nations reserves: poll," *National Post,* January 15, 2013; Michael

Harris, "When native-bashing became good politics," *ipolitics.ca,* March 24, 2013.

6. Shawn Atleo, "The Economics of Reconciliation," speech given to the Canadian Club of Toronto, April 23, 2012, *www.afn.ca/uploads/files/nc/notescdnclub.pdf.* See also, Adrian Humphry, "Corporate Canada should embrace First Nations as full partners in resource development says Chief Shawn Atleo," *National Post,* April 23, 2012.

7. See, for example, Chief Ghislain Pecard, who declared during the 2014 Quebec provincial elections, "We have a right to self-determination and this right is not negotiable." Benjamin Shingler, "First Nations on Quebec sovereignty debate: We decide out own future," Canadian Press, March 15, 2014.

8. Melanie Patten, "Elsipogtog First Nation Sees Violence As RCMP Moves To End Protest," Canadian Press, January 23, 2014.

9. Of unique interest and vulnerability is Winnipeg's complete dependence for fresh water on a pipeline that runs from Shoal Lake located within an area claimed by the Iskatewizaagegan First Nation in Ontario through a completely exposed, unguarded, 156-kilometre pipeline into reservoirs near the city.

10. This list of vulnerable "bottlenecks" is taken in abbreviated form from Douglas L. Bland, *Canada and The First Nations: Cooperation or Conflict,* Aboriginal Canada and the Natural Resource Economy: 2 (Ottawa: Macdonald-Laurier Institute, May 2013), 23.

11. *Ibid.,* 19–24.

12. Susan Taylor, "CN reaches deal with union," *National Post,* February 3, 2014.

13. "Japan turns to U.S. wheat after shipments from Canada delayed." *National Post,* February 7, 2014.

14. Vanessa Lu, "Canadian farmers sitting on grain due to railway logjam," *Toronto Star,* February 12, 2014.

15. "Sask. sends cabinet ministers to meet with companies about grain backlog," *Global News,* February 12, 2014.

16. Claudia Cattaneo, "XL effect spread to farms," *National Post,* February 13, 2014.

17. "Update 3 — Canada orders railways to boost grain shipments to ease logjam," *www.reuters.com,* March 7, 2014.

18. Canada, The Integrated Terrorism Assessment Centre is intended to bring "… together the various participants in Canada's security intelligence community — from the Canadian Security Intelligence Service (CSIS) to police forces — to provide the Government of Canada with the information required to take action to

prevent or reduce the effects and threat of terrorism on Canadians." "*Public Safety Canada* was created in 2003 to ensure coordination across all federal departments and agencies responsible for national security and the safety of Canadians."

19. See, for instance, Michael Harris, "Think the aboriginal rage has cooled? Think again," *iPolitics*, March 14, 2013; Michael Woods, "CN Rail's blockade frustration revealed," *National Post*, April 13, 2013; Alexandra Paul, "Court blocks CN blockaders," *Winnipeg Free Press*, October 7, 2013; Matthew Pearson, "Four arrested as native blockade causes Via Rail delays," *Ottawa Citizen*, March 8, 2014; and "VIA Rail blockade by First Nations halts Montreal–Toronto trains," *CBC News*, March 19, 2014.

20. Derek Nepinak, "New First Nations Education Act an 'illusion of control,'" *CBC News*, April 11, 2014, *www.cbc.ca/news*.

21. Peter O'Neil, "Rift among First Nations leaders over threat for 'economic shutdown' coast to coast," *National Post*, May 16, 2014.

22. "Valcourt attacks Confederacy of Nations, calls chief 'rogue' and threat to national security," *APTN National News*, May 16, 2014, *http://aptn.ca/news*.

23. Pamela Palmater, "CSIS and me: What First Nation activities are NOT considered

a potential threat to Canada?" *Rabble* (January 5, 2012). Emphasis in the original.

CHAPTER 7

1. Atleo, "The Economics of Reconciliation," 2.

2. Harry Swain, *Oka: A Political Crisis And Its Legacy* (Vancouver: Douglas & McIntyre, 2010), 204.

3. *Ibid.*, 205.

4. For a play on the notion, see, Thomas King, *The Inconvenient Indian: A Curious Account of Native People in North America* (Toronto: Doubleday Canada, 2012), 70–71.

5. Tom Flanagan, *Beyond the Indian Act* (Montreal and Kingston: McGill-Queen's University Press, 2010). For a brief critique of Flanagan's views, see, King, *The Inconvenient Indian,* 199.

6. Alia Dharssi, "Saskatchewan band becomes first of First Nations to take full control of natural resources," *National Post*, March 22, 2014.

7. *Ibid.*

8. Canada, AANDC, "Treaties with Aboriginal people in Canada," September 15, 2010, *www.aadnc-aandc.gc.ca/eng/110 0100032291/1100100032292*.

9. *Ibid.* The first of these modern-day treaties was the James Bay and Northern Quebec Agreement, signed in 1975.

10. Canada, AANDC, "Progress Report — Specific Claims 2012–2013." August 18, 2013, *www.aadnc-aandc.gc.ca/eng/1339507365950/1339507443870*. Not all claims assessments and negotiations result in settlements in favour of a First Nation's claim. A claim may be considered "concluded" when it is "not accepted" by the federal government or when a First Nation takes "not action on the claim."

11. Canada, AANDC, "Treaties with Aboriginal people in Canada."

12. Treaty Land Entitlement Implementation Monitoring Committee of Manitoba, "Message from Chief Genaille," in *Annual Report: 2012–2013*, 5.

13. Canada, AANDC, "The Government of Canada's Approach to Implementation of the Inherent Right and the Negotiation of Aboriginal Self-Government: Part I — Policy framework," September 15, 2009.

14. *Ibid.*

15. *Ibid.*

16. Some readers might suggest that this entire essay and the some of the author's other writings are based on an imagined First Nations national security problem and, insofar as the novel *Uprising* is concerned, there is some truth to that claim. In self-defence, I suggest that my work is not aimed at declaring a national security danger requiring an urgent armed police or military response. It is, however, intended to warn Canadians and the First Nations people that there is a public security aspect to our relationship that if left untended or placed in the hands of various security services might well create the very situation they had intended to prevent.

17. Justin Ling, "Canada's Spy agency helped prepare all-of-government approach in case *Idle No More* protests 'escalated': secret files," *National Post*, March 23, 2014. See also, "CSIS, Aboriginal Affairs kept close watch on Idle No More protest movement," Postmedia News, August 11, 2013.

18. *Ibid.*

CHAPTER 8

1. Harry Swain, *Oka: A Political Crisis and Its Legacy* (Vancouver: Douglas & McIntyre, 2010), 202.

2. For example, see Dene Moore, "Yinka Dene say their decision is final: Northern Gateway pipeline officially rejected," Canadian Press, April 11, 2014. Also, "Kitimat, B.C. votes 'no' to Northern Gateway in plebiscite," *CBC News*, April 12, 2014.

3. Henry E. Eccles, *Military Concepts and Philosophy* (New Brunswick, NJ: Rutgers University Press, 1965), 83.

4. For a fuller discussion of these "feasibility determinants" in a Canadian context, see, Douglas L. Bland, *Canada and The First Nations: Cooperation or Conflict*, Aboriginal Canada and the Natural Resource Economy: 2 (Ottawa: Macdonald-Laurier Institute, May 2013).

5. Ben Connable and Martin C. Libicki, *How Insurgencies End* (Santa Monica, CA: Rand Corporation, 2010), xi.

6. *Ibid.*, 2.

7. *Ibid.*, xvii.

8. *Ibid.*, xvi.

9. *Ibid.*

10. *Ibid.*

11. *Ibid.*, 2.

12. *Ibid.*

13. *Ibid.*

14. *Ibid.*, xii.

15. *Ibid.*

16. *Ibid.*, xv.

17. *Ibid.*, xvii.

18. Christie Blatchford, *Helpless: Caledonia's Nightmare of Fear and Anarchy, and How the Law failed Them* (Toronto: Doubleday Canada, 2010); and also Harry Swain, *Oka: A Political Crisis and Its Legacy* (Vancouver: Douglas & McIntyre, 2010), 100–02.

19. Assembly of First Nations, "Charter of the Assembly of First Nations, Ideals."

20. Jason Fekete, "Stephen Harper meets with First Nations as sprawling protest unfolds in Ottawa," *National Post*, January 11, 2013. See also, Gloria Galloway, "Harper, chiefs to meet amid chaos, protests," *Globe and Mail*, January 10, 2013.

21. "Theresa Spence pulls out of meeting with Harper," *CBC News*, January 9, 2013.

22. The credibility of this concept is supported by research suggesting — whether because of official policies or some other reasons — that "44 percent of 18- to 24-year-olds who have left [life on-reserve] do not plan to go back to their home communities. Another 33 percent are undecided." The research also noted (2001–2011) that the on-reserve population of 20- to 24-year-olds has declined significantly and the trend is continuing: Ally Quinney, "Brain drain challenges First Nation communities across Canada," *CBC News*, April 16, 2014. Also, "Urban Aboriginal People Study," Environics, 2009.

23. Canada, Clerk of the Privy Council, "First Nations Control of First Nations Education Act," February 7, 2014.

24. Canada, AANDC, "Backgrounder: First Nations Control of First Nations Education Act," March 10, 2014.

25. *Ibid.*

26. "Shawn Atleo: First Nations Education Act 'must act as

bridge,'" *CBC News*, April 12, 2014.

27. See also, Susanna Mas, "Aboriginal education bill meets First Nations conditions: Bernard Valcourt," *CBC News*, April 10, 2014. Also, Gloria Galloway, "Atleo under fire for support of Conservative native-education measures" *Globe and Mail*, April 11, 2014.

28. Derek Nepinak, "New First Nations Education Act an 'illusion of control,'" *CBC News*, April 14, 2014.

29. Some chiefs suggested that they will do "whatever is necessary" to disrupt the federal government's First Nations' education policies. See, "Chiefs vow to do whatever it takes to scrap Aboriginal education bill," Canadian Press, April 28, 2014, *www. cbc.ca/news/ Aboriginal chiefs*. In the same statement, however, Chief Nepinak seemed to back away from those chiefs who "… think (the) Canadian economy, eventually, will be a target."

30. Joseph Brean, "Atleo's resignation does more than derail the $1.9B First Nations education plan, it may have upended the whole AFN," *National Post*, May 6, 2014.

31. Chief Phil Fontaine, as quoted on *CTV News*, May 15, 2007.

32. Jorge Barrera and Kenneth Jackson, "Rail blockades marches, highway shutdowns planned for Wednesday," *APTN News*, January 14, 2013, *www.aptn.ca/ news/2013*.

33. Brian Lee Crowley and Ken Coates, "New Beginnings: How Canada's Natural Resources Wealth Could Re-shape Relations with Aboriginal People," Aboriginal Canada and the Natural Resource Economy Series: 1 (Ottawa: Macdonald-Laurier Institute, May 2013), 1.

34. Brian Lee Crowley and Ken Coates, "The Way Out: New thinking about Aboriginal engagements and the energy infrastructure to the West Coast," Aboriginal Canada and the Natural Resource Economy Series: 1 (Ottawa: Macdonald-Laurier Institute, May 2013), 1.

35. *Ibid.*, 7.

36. Les Whittington, "First Nations leaders want in on natural resources boom," *Toronto Star*, January 11, 2013.

37. Frances Widdowson, "A 'dream palace' built on gas and gold won't solve Aboriginal poverty," *Globe and Mail*, January 10, 2013.

EPILOGUE

1. Chief Terry Nelson, as quoted on *CTV News*, May 15, 2007.

Douglas Bland served for thirty years as a senior officer in the Canadian Armed Forces, then as Chair of Defence Studies at Queen's University. He is the author of the acclaimed novel *Uprising* as well as numerous essays on Canadian and international security affairs. He lives in Kingston, Ontario.